ON THE MOVE

AN ENCYCLOPEDIA OF TRANSPORT

MARSHALL PUBLISHING • LONDON

A Marshall Edition

Produced by *Kinsey* & **Harrison** for
Marshall Editions Ltd
The Orangery, 161 New Bond Street
London W1S 2UF
www.marshallpublishing.com

First published in the UK in 2001 by
Marshall Publishing Ltd

Copyright © 2001 Marshall Editions Developments Ltd

ISBN 1 84028 453 6

Originated in Singapore by PICA
Printed and bound in Portugal by Printer Portuguesa

10 9 8 7 6 5 4 3 2 1

General Consultant: (and *Wheels* and *Air*)
Andrew Nahum, Senior Curator, Aeronautics and Road Transport, Science Museum, London
Contributors: Philip Wilkinson, Ian Graham, Howard Johnston, Ian Ward
Consultants: *Tracks*: Tim Bryan, Steam: Museum of the Great Western Railway, Swindon; *Water*: Pieter van der Merwe, General Editor, National Maritime Museum, Greenwich; *Space*: Douglas Millard, Associate Curator, Space Technology, Science Museum, London
Indexer: Patricia Hymans

Designer: Edward Kinsey Editor: James Harrison

Marshall Editions
Design Managers: Ralph Pitchford, Caroline Sangster
Editorial Manager: Kate Phelps
Assistant Editor: Elise See Tai
Proofreader: Claire Sipi
Picture Researcher: Zilda Tandy
Production: Christina Schuster

Contents

Introduction

Since the earliest times, people have travelled – to find food, to carry goods for trading, for sheer adventure, to find out what is over the next hill or to find new lands across the sea. To begin with, they walked or rode animals, but they built the first boats in prehistoric times, and wheeled vehicles were first used 5,000 years ago.

For thousands of years these forms of transport developed gradually. Boat-builders designed better sails and methods of steering their craft; different styles of cart and carriage were developed for land transport. These changes came slowly, but they had a huge effect. For example, better ships enabled people such as the Vikings to go on the first long-distance voyages of exploration, crossing the Atlantic in search of new places to settle. Again in the 15th and 16th centuries, European explorers used the latest ships to go huge distances, some even sailing right around the globe. But few people travelled that far. Most men and women did not go far beyond their immediate neighbourhood, and if they did travel long distances, the journey was likely to be slow, difficult and dangerous.

Woodburner

Then, in the 19th century, a change took place which transformed transport for good. Engineers in Europe developed the railways, bringing fast, safe land transport within the reach of many people for the first time.

The railways also allowed goods to be transported faster and more efficiently than ever before, helping industry and making people less reliant on food and other items produced near home.

Rapid transport, rapid change

By the beginning of the 20th century, the next leap forward in the story of transport had taken place. The first cars were on the road and the first aeroplanes were in the air. Suddenly, the world seemed a smaller place and the pace of change got faster. Cars became cheaper and better designed; aircraft grew in size and got faster; ocean liners became more luxurious and cargo vessels got bigger. In every area of transport, engines were made both more powerful and more efficient and there were improvements in comfort and safety.

Today in the developed world,

Viking longship

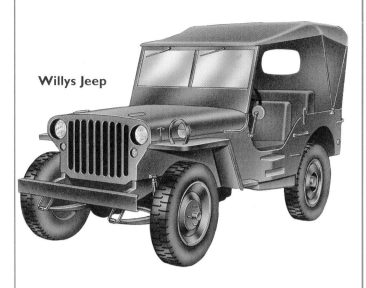

Willys Jeep

many families own at least one car and regular air travel is a reality. In 1961 the Russians amazed the world by sending the first person into space.

By the end of the 1960s, men had walked on the Moon and in the next decade unmanned space probes were sent far out into the solar system. Nearer the ground, the supersonic airliner *Concorde* had cut down the journey time between London and New York to a mere three hours.

Travelling in the future

In the future, transport on the ground and at sea may also become much swifter, with faster trains, cars and ships on the drawing board. But governments and manufacturers are trying to make transport more efficient, so that we use less of the world's precious resources as we travel around. There are already exciting experimental boats and cars powered by the sun's rays, and many scientists hope that the fuel cell, already used in some spacecraft, will one day provide quiet, efficient, low energy power for many other vehicles. Meanwhile, designers

are always coming up with ways of making cars, trains, boats and planes more streamlined, to cut down drag and get more speed with less fuel. The resulting vehicles perform better, and often look amazing too.

How to use this book

This book is divided into five easy-to-follow sections dealing with transport on the road, in the water, on railways, in the air and in space. Within each section, most of the pages contain a series of catalogue-style entries on a range of craft and vehicles. Each entry contains the story of the vehicle and a fact box to see at-a-glance aspects from speed and size to the number of people carried. In addition, each section contains feature pages that deal with especially interesting topics, such as Formula One racing, high-speed trains or developments in low-energy transport. Finally, at the back of the book you will find fact-packed lists on famous people, amazing transport facts, what the technical terms mean and a timeline of transport history.

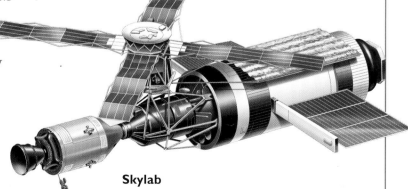

Skylab

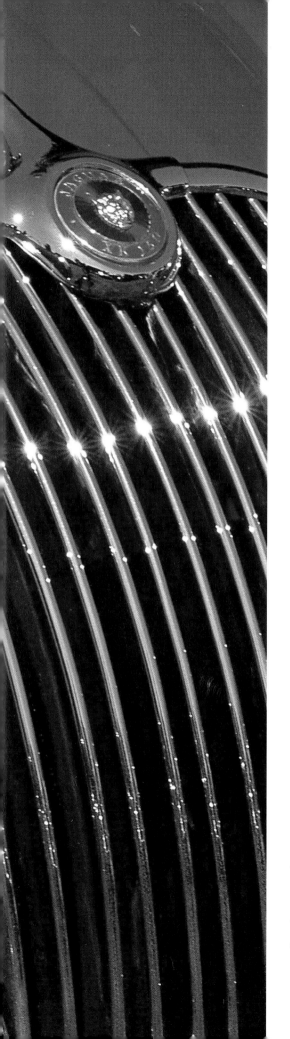

On wheels

Long before the invention of the motor car there was plenty of road transport – chariots, stagecoaches, Hansom cabs and other vehicles. Bumpy roads made long journeys uncomfortable, but they were possible.

When the motor car was invented at the end of the 19th century some people tried to ban it, and to control its speed so it did not frighten the horses. Early laws even required someone to walk ahead waving a red flag, although this was often hard to enforce. However, the motor car grew in popularity. In 1908 the first mass-produced car, the American Model T Ford, opened up the prospect of cheap transport for everyone. By 1922 there were 2 million Model Ts alone, and by the year 2000, 35 million cars were being produced each year.

Morris Cowley "Bullnose"

With his **Morris Cowley** and **Morris Oxford** "Bullnose" family cars, William Morris brought mass motoring to Britain in the 1920s. At that time there was also, and still is, a demand for luxury cars – *Jaguar* has been famous for producing luxury sports cars and sports saloons, like the MkII (*left*).

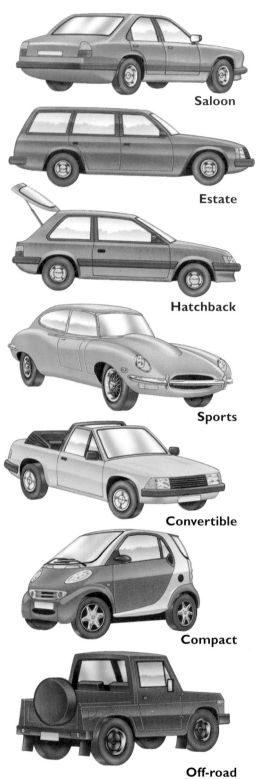

Saloon

Estate

Hatchback

Sports

Convertible

Compact

Off-road

What is a car?

The wheel was invented over 5,000 years ago, but the car has only been around for 100 years. In that short time this vehicle has changed the way we live and move about. How would we manage without this handy form of transport that has developed from being a basic horseless carriage to a high-tech road machine?

Parts of a car

Nearly all cars have four wheels, each one has a spring and damper to absorb the bumps. The engine is usually at the front and is usually mounted sideways. It drives the front wheels only. Car bodies are made of steel, aluminium or plastic.

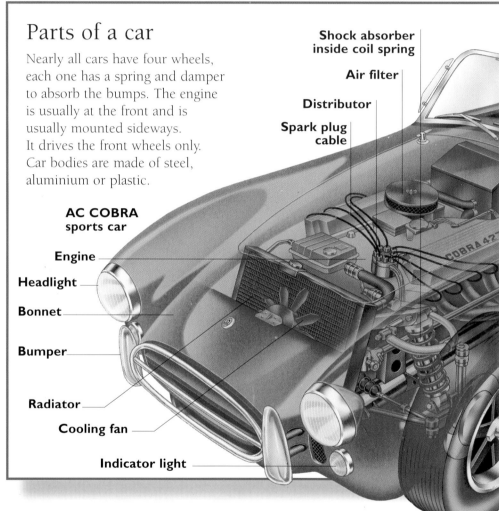

AC COBRA sports car

Engine

Headlight

Bonnet

Bumper

Radiator

Cooling fan

Indicator light

Shock absorber inside coil spring

Air filter

Distributor

Spark plug cable

COBRA 427

Stretched

People carrier

Car types

The cars (*left*) show the amazing variety of shapes and sizes available today – from seven-seater people carriers to two-seater sports convertibles. Compact cars are for the city, while off-road vehicles can tackle the roughest wild tracks.

Tyre types

All tyres are round and black. Standard tyres have some grooves to clear water away, but off-road versions are very knobbly, to grip better in mud. Old tyres were very narrow and had little grip.

High drag   Low drag

Aerodynamics (airflow)

Car designers and engineers use wind tunnels to check a car's aerodynamics. A ribbon of smoke is blasted along the tunnel and this ribbon flows over the car showing if it has a smooth shape with low "drag", which means more speed for less fuel. Aerodynamic studies are also used to make cars stable on the road at speed.

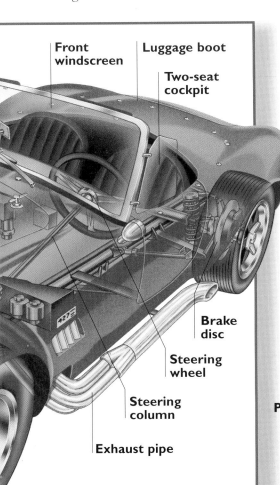

Front windscreen
Luggage boot
Two-seat cockpit
Brake disc
Steering wheel
Steering column
Exhaust pipe

How engines work

Petrol engines have cylinders with pistons going up and down inside them. The pistons are driven down by a mixture of petrol and oil burning quickly above them. The up and down movement is turned into rotation by connecting rods linking the pistons to the crankshaft. The crankshaft is joined to the wheels of the car by the clutch and the gearbox. The camshaft (controls) opens and closes the valves to let in the correct fuel and air mixture and to let the exhaust gases out of the cylinder.

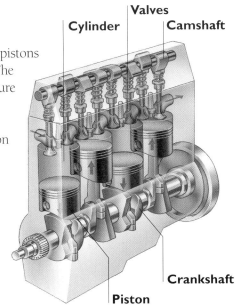

Cylinder
Valves
Camshaft
Crankshaft
Piston

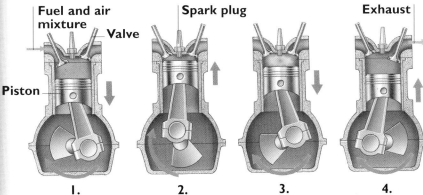

Fuel and air mixture
Valve
Piston
Spark plug
Exhaust

1.   2.   3.   4.

Early solid rubber
Early air-filled
Standard grooves
Racing (no grooves)

The four-stroke cycle

Most engines run on the four-stroke or Otto cycle. As a piston moves down the cylinder, a valve opens to allow the fuel and air mixture to be sucked in (**1**). As the piston starts to rise again, the valve closes and the mixture is compressed (**2**). Near the top of the piston stroke, a spark plug ignites the mixture, which burns quickly and expands to push the piston down again (**3**). Near the bottom once more, another valve opens to allow the rising piston to force the waste "exhaust" gas out (**4**). Then the cycle starts again.

9

Before engines

Once people discovered how to roll rather than slide things, transport became much easier. By 3000 BC, domesticated animals were harnessed to pull carts, the designs of which were to improve over the centuries. There were experiments using sails and even clockwork motors, but oxen were the most common.

Roman chariot

Country: Italy
Date: c.200 BC
Size: 4.2 m (13¼ ft) long
Body: wood
Top speed: 24 km/h (15 mph)
On board: 1 or 2

Oxen farm cart

Country: Europe
Date: 1100s
Size: 3 m (10 ft) long
Body: wood
Top speed: 5 km/h (3 mph)
On board: 0

Roman chariot

Chariots were pulled by two, three or four horses, and the one or two passengers used to stand. The Roman army used chariots to transport spear carriers and archers. Fighting chariots even had sharp blades attached to the wheels. Chariot racing was very popular.

Oxen farm cart

After the invention of the wheel (see page 42), sledges were modified into simple carts. In the 1100s, these carts were used for farm work, with oxen to pull them. Each cart could carry much more produce at one time than ever before.

Chinese wheelbarrow

Wheelbarrows were first used in China around 200 AD. They were different from modern garden barrows because they had the load over the wheel rather than behind it, which made them easier to lift. Some barrows even had sails to help them along.

Chinese wheelbarrow

Country: China
Date: c.200 AD
Size: 1.5 m (5 ft) long
Body: wood with fabric sail
Top speed: 4 km/h (2½ mph)
On board: 0

Country: Europe
Date: 1600s
Size: 3.4 m (11 ft) long
Body: wood
Top speed: 2 km/h (1¼ mph)
On board: 2

Treadmill carriage

Treadmill carriage

One of many attempts at replacing animals to pull carts was this self-propelled carriage. It was steered by rope, and power came from the man at the back "walking" on a tread wheel that made the rear axle turn. In fact it would have been easier to push the vehicle along, and the vehicle was a failure.

Hansom cab

Country: UK
Date: 1834
Size: 1.8 m (6 ft) long
Body: wooden body and wheels, with iron tyres
Top speed: 10 km/h (6½ mph)
On board: 2 plus driver

Hansom cab

John Hansom invented this light and elegant two-wheeled cab. It was a common sight in Victorian London. The driver stood at the back and on top of the cab, and he could talk to his passengers through a trap door in the roof. There was a folding door at the front and a bench seat above the two wheels.

Concorde stagecoach

By 1802, Americans could travel the 1,900 km (1,200 miles) from Boston to Savannah in "stages" by different coaches. The best known stagecoach was the *Concorde*, of which nearly 4,000 were made. They carried passengers inside with a driver and guard on top with the luggage. Leather springs made the ride more comfortable, with greater speed given by six horses.

Concorde stagecoach

Country: USA
Date: 1830
Size: 3.7 m (12 ft) long
Body: wood with leather springs, metal strengthening
Top speed: 24 km/h (15 mph)
On board: 6 plus 2 crew

Country: USA
Date: 1850s
Size: 3.7 m (12 ft) long
Body: wood
Top speed: 6 km/h (3¾ mph)
On board: 2 or 3

Covered wagon

Canvas-covered wagons were the caravans or trailers of the 1850s. Some 55,000 US settlers used them to head west, often in groups called wagon trains. The wooden frames could carry several tonnes, and were usually hauled by oxen or mules – often in teams of six – and could only manage about 30 km (20 miles) a day.

Covered wagon

The first cars

In 1769 French army officer Nicholas Cugnot built the first self-propelled steam vehicle – a tractor to pull army guns – but it crashed into a wall. About 100 years later Karl Benz and Gottlieb Daimler developed the first crude petrol-engined buggies. These first cars were unreliable and could barely reach 15 km/h (9 mph). Nevertheless, the "horseless" carriage was overtaking the horse and carriage, and soon the first modern-looking cars appeared with engines mounted at the front.

La Mancelle

Country: France
Date: 1878
Size: 4 m (13 ft) long
Body: wood and steel
Top speed: 10 km/h (6.5 mph)
On board: 6 plus firearm at rear

Benz "Motorwagen"

The first workable car, named after its inventor Karl Benz, was a three-wheeled vehicle with a tubular steel frame and an open wooden two-seater body. The single front wheel was steered by a tiller, while the two larger rear wheels were driven by chains. The petrol engine was mounted horizontally at the back between the rear wheels.

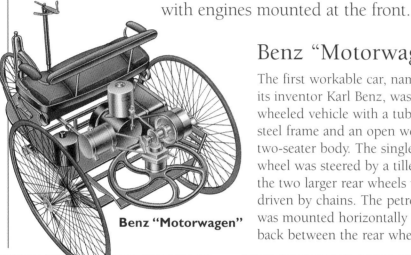

Benz "Motorwagen"

La Mancelle

Amédée Bollée's *La Mancelle* steamer set the style for motor cars to come. It featured a front-mounted engine driving the rear wheels, and a steering shaft, gearbox and rods to swivel the wheels. Though not fast, *La Mancelle* ("The Girl from Le Mans") did knock down a horse.

Country: Germany
Date: 1885/86
Size: 2.5 m (8 ft) long
Body: wood and steel
Top speed: 13 km/h (8 mph)
On board: 2

Country: Germany
Date: 1893
Size: 2.5 m (8 ft) long
Body: wood and steel
Top speed: 25 km/h (15 mph)
On board: 2

Benz Viktoria

The *Viktoria* was the first four-wheeler from Karl Benz, one of the most famous names in the motor industry. It was also the first car to carry a model name, and an accurate steering system using a crude steering wheel rather than a tiller or lever. The *Viktoria* was also the first car to go into proper production. However, it still looked like a cart that had lost its horses.

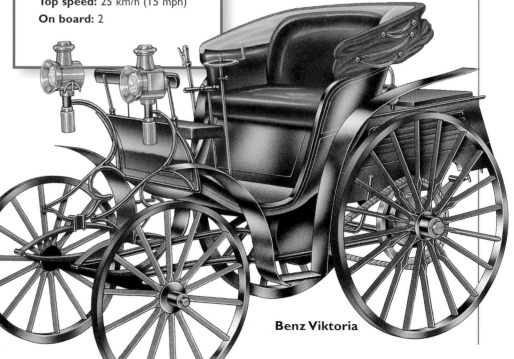

Benz Viktoria

Panhard-Levassor

Stanley Model 71

Panhard-Levassor

Early French car-makers René Panhard and Emile Levassor designed a car that set the standard for other car-makers to follow: a front-mounted engine, the gearbox in the middle and rear wheel drive.

Country: France
Date: 1894
Size: 2.5 m (8 ft) long
Body: wood and steel
Top speed: 20 km/h (12½ mph)
On board: 4

Oldsmobile Curved Dash

Country: USA
Date: 1910
Size: 3.5 m (11½ ft) long
Body: steel and wood
Top speed: 88 km/h (55 mph)
On board: 4

Stanley Model 71

Steam power was still a serious rival to petrol in the early days of motoring. The American Stanley twins built successful mass-produced steam cars right into the 1920s. This 20 horsepower tourer had its boiler mounted under the front bonnet and the engine at the back driving the rear wheels.

Oldsmobile Curved Dash

Named after the shape of the footboard at the front, the *Curved Dash* was the world's first mass-produced car. A factory fire destroyed all the drawings, but the first model survived and 4,000 copies were made at the Ransom E Olds factory in Lansing, Michigan, USA from 1901 to 1905. Hundreds of parts were made and assembled there to complete each car.

Renault Buggy

Louis, Marcel and Fernand Renault founded one of the most famous French car making companies. Their first cars used de Dion engines and this early model had a 1¼ horsepower engine under a half-rounded bonnet in the front driving the rear wheels. Renault also produced one of the first cars with a completely enclosed body.

Country: USA
Date: 1901
Size: 2.5 m (8 ft) long
Body: wood and steel
Top speed: 32 km/h (20 mph)
On board: 2

Renault Buggy

Country: France
Date: 1899
Size: 3 m (10 ft) long
Body: wood and steel
Top speed: 20 km/h (12½ mph)
On board: 4

Mean machines

There are some wheeled vehicles that stand out from the crowd. They are bigger, heavier, taller, longer or faster than anything else. Some may have been "customised" – like hot-rod cars "sunk" low and fitted with extra wide wheels and a powerful racing-tuned engine, or "stretched limos" with extra chassis and wheels to allow passengers to stretch out and enjoy television, a refrigerator and bar. Some are built for sport, others to carry important people safely with bullet- and bomb-proofing, and some to beat a speed or endurance record.

Bigfoot

Bigfoot began as a pick-up truck with big tyres and suspension for car crushing displays at fairs. The tyres are over 1.8 m (6 ft) high. *Bigfoots* have powerful engines and lightweight bodies to set long jump records of over 62 m (200 ft).

Bigfoot

Country: USA
Date: 1976
Size: 5.5 m (18 ft) long
Body: alloys on a tubular frame
Top speed: 100 km/h (65½ mph)
On board: 2

AEC Mammoth Major

This 1960s "road-train" was specially built in Australia by the British AEC company. It could carry 100 tonnes of goods at a time across the vast Australian outback (where there are no railways). Throwing up clouds of dust, it resembled a fast-moving crocodile in the sand.

AEC Mammoth Major

CAUTION
LONG FREIGHTER STOCK TRUCK

Country: Australia
Date: 1960
Size: 45 m (148 ft) long with 3 trailers
Body: steel and alloys
Top speed: 88 km/h (55 mph)
On board: 3

Thrust SSC

This was the first car to break the sound barrier, at Black Rock Desert, USA, in July 1997. Driven by Andy Green, it took just 4.67 seconds to pass through the measured mile. At the record speed, the big aluminium wheels rotate 8,500 times a minute and the parachutes released to slow down the vehicle give 10 tonnes of braking force.

Thrust SSC

Country: UK
Date: 1997
Size: 14.6 m (47¾ ft) long
Body: steel frame, aluminium panels
Top speed: 1221 km/h (763 mph)
On board: 1

Dragster

This dragster's huge engine is tuned to produce 6,000 horsepower for the four seconds it takes to pass through a measured mile. The front steering wheels are tiny, but the back tyres are huge because they have to drive the dragster. The driver sits just behind the engine, which is cooled by ice and runs on an alcohol based fuel.

Dragster

Country: USA
Date: 2000
Size: 6 m (19¾ ft) long
Body: steel frame, some composite panelling
Top speed: 320 km/h (200 mph)
On board: 1

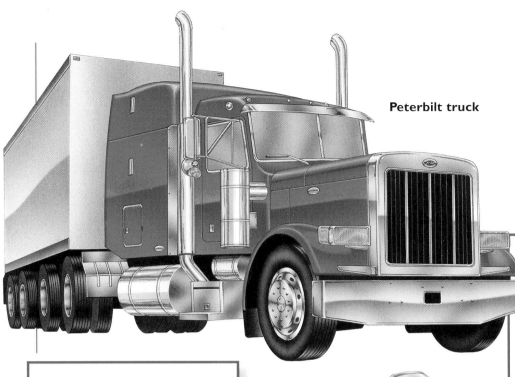

Peterbilt truck

Peterbilt truck

With their chrome exhaust stacks pointing to the sky, such huge "long-nosed" or bonneted trucks haul loads of more than 40 tonnes across America. These massive transporters are built to travel several million kilometres in their lifetime.

Country: USA
Date: 1990s
Size: 12.2 m (40 ft) long
Body: steel frame with aluminium cab
Top speed: 96 km/h (60 mph)
On board: 2 or 3

Country: USA
Date: 1990
Size: about 4 m (13 ft) long
Body: AIV (aluminium intensive vehicle) frame and panels
Top speed: 230 km/h (143 mph)
On board: 2

Panoz AIV Roadster

Panoz AIV roadster

Looking like a 1950s hot rod, the *Panoz* has a powerful V8 engine delivering 305 horsepower. It can go from 0 to 100 km/h (0–60 mph) in 4.6 seconds. Each car takes 350 hours to hand build and many of the parts are developed from racing cars.

Country: USA
Date: 1982
Size: 4.6 m (15 ft) long
Body: steel and alloys
Top speed: 128 km/h (80 mph)
On board: Up to 10

Hummer HMMWV

The *Hummer* was designed for the American army as a go-anywhere vehicle. The initials HMMWV stand for High Mobility Multi-Purpose Wheeled Vehicle, sometimes shortened to the name *Humvee*. Today it is very popular for civilian use. With four-wheel drive, it can climb up incredibly steep hills at 11 km/h (7 mph) and can go through up to 1.5 m (5 ft) of water. It can do 0 to 80 km/h (0–50 mph) in 14 seconds. Customised versions include one with caterpillar tracks.

Hummer HMMWV

Luxury cars

The bodies of the first cars were hand-built from the finest timbers, and hand-painted with fully upholstered seats, carpets and curtains – reflecting the luxury of horse-drawn carriages before them. The 1920s saw the coachmaker's craft at its peak with royalty and movie stars demanding leather seats, walnut dashboards and even gold or silver plating. The luxury car market continues today with features such as multimedia consoles and space-age navigation systems.

Delage D8

Bugatti 41 Royale

Known as the "Golden Bug", the gigantic *Bugatti Royale* was so large that a *Mini* (see page 20) could be parked on its bonnet. Designed for monarchs, only six examples were sold. The engines later found use in high-speed French railcars.

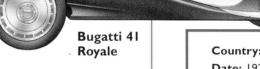

Bugatti 41 Royale

Country: France
Date: 1926
Size: 6.7 m (22 ft) long
Body: steel
Top speed: 160 km/h (100 mph)
On board: 6

Country: France
Date: 1930
Size: from 4.8 m (16 ft) long
Body: steel
Top speed: 160 km/h (100 mph)
On board: 2 to 6 depending on body style

Delage D8

Louis Delage started building cars in 1906 and in 1912 he sold 1,000 vehicles. His cars were successful in the first international road races – one model won the Indianapolis "500" in 1914. The luxury tourer *D8* could manage 0 to 100 km/h (0–60 mph) in about 15 seconds, while the *D8SS* sports version averaged 180 km/h (112 mph) during 12 hours in trials.

Hispano-Suiza H6-B

Designed by Swiss engineer Mark Birkigt, this was the most technically advanced car in the world from 1919 to 1938. Hispano also made aircraft engines, and they developed a six-cylinder engine for this car as well as advanced four-wheel brakes.

Country: France
Date: 1919
Size: 4.8 m (16 ft) long
Body: steel
Top speed: 137 km/h (85 mph)
On board: 2 to 6 depending on body style

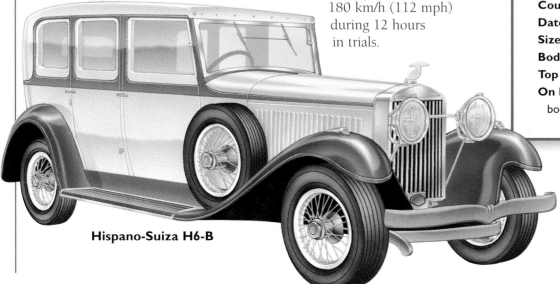

Hispano-Suiza H6-B

Silver Ghost

Silver Ghost

Rolls-Royce's elegant luxury car, the *40/50 hp* (hp for horsepower), was so quiet it earned the name "Silver Ghost". One model actually had silver-plated fittings, and this model was produced for 19 years with a variety of elegant bodies to suit individual owners.

Country: UK
Date: from 1906
Size: from 4.7 m (15½ ft) long
Body: steel
Top speed: 85 km/h (53 mph)
On board: 4

Mercedes Benz S-Class

With a sleeker body than before, this top-of-the-range "Merc" had just about every possible accessory, together with all kinds of electronic wizardry, such as rain-sensing windscreen wipers and electric seats with built-in memory.

Country: USA
Date: 1974
Size: 6 m (20 ft) long
Body: steel
Top speed: 192 km/h (120 mph)
On board: 6

Lincoln Town Car

Mercedes Benz S-Class

Lincoln Town Car

Lincoln is still the Ford motor company's American luxury brand. It started as an independent company in the 1920s and was named after the founder's hero, President Lincoln. This 1970s *Town Car* had a distinctive coffin-shaped bonnet and retractable headlights. Its great size was typical of American saloons of the time as was the "gas-guzzling" 7.5-litre V8 engine.

Country: Germany
Date: 1999
Size: 5.1 m (16½ ft) long
Body: steel
Top speed: from 232 km/h (145 mph)
On board: 5

Country: Japan
Date: 1998
Size: 5 m (16¼ ft) long
Body: steel
Top speed: 230 km/h (143 mph)
On board: 5

Lexus GS300

Lexus is the name the Japanese Toyota company uses for its luxury range of cars. The *GS300* has a powerful six-cylinder engine and a satellite navigation system that has voice instructions to guide the driver to his or her destination.

Lexus GS300

People movers

The earliest cars could often seat four people, but the price was too high for the average family. It was only when Henry Ford put his famous *Model T* into mass (factory) production that family motoring became a real possibility. Since then this type of car, with plenty of seats and doors, has been the most popular, with many manufacturers competing hard to win sales. Today, "people carriers" have become very fashionable, particularly for larger families, but medium-sized saloons are as much in demand as ever.

Model T Ford

Morris Cowley

Morris Cowley

William Morris left school at 15, repaired bicycles and cars and bought a garage in Oxford, England. From 1913 to 1926 his *Cowley* was a rival to the American *Model T Ford*. Also called "bullnose" (because of the shape of the radiator) over 50,000 of these family cars were sold.

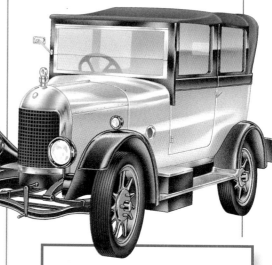

Country: UK
Date: 1913
Size: 3.7 m (12 ft) long
Body: steel
Top speed: 80 km/h (50 mph)
On board: 2 to 4 depending on body style

Model T Ford

"Any colour as long as it's black" was one of the sayings for which car maker Henry Ford was famous. It applied to his *Model T Ford*, which introduced machine-made cars for the masses for the first time. Between 1908 and 1927, more than 15 million *Model Ts* were made. Such was the speed of production that there was no time to paint cars different colours at first.

Country: USA
Date: 1908
Size: from 3.5 m (1½ ft) long
Body: steel
Top speed: 72 km/h (45 mph)
On board: 2 to 4 depending on body style

Volkswagen Beetle

This simple but innovative car, with its air-cooled engine, was designed by Dr Ferdinand Porsche (see page 22) in 1936. He was responding to the German government's demand for a *volkswagen* ("people's car"). Although many thought it ugly, it became the best-selling car of all time.

Volkswagen Beetle

Country: Germany
Date: 1939
Size: 4 m (13 ft) long
Body: steel
Top speed: 100 km/h (60 mph)
On board: 4

Rambler Ambassador

Country: USA
Date: 1958
Size: 5.5 m (18 ft) long
Body: steel
Top speed: 160 km/h
(100 mph)
On board: 6

Rambler Ambassador

Huge bonnets, high tail fins, plenty of chrome-plated steel and big, thirsty V8 engines were common in 1950s American family cars. It was a "glamour" look. The *Ambassador* had four doors but no fixed support between the side windows.

Country: France
Date: 1961
Size: 3.6 m (12 ft) long
Body: steel
Top speed: 112 km/h
(70 mph)
On board: 4

Renault 4

Renault 4

Renault President Pierre Dreyfus dreamed of a car for all types of people, what he called the "Blue Jeans Car", and the Renault 4 was the result. Rugged, basic and inexpensive, it performed well on all types of terrain and with five doors it provided compact family transport. Six million were sold.

Rover 75

Despite good press reviews, which can influence people's purchasing decisions, the 75 sold poorly. Rover got into trouble and the owners BMW sold the company. The styling has a solid, old-fashioned Rover look, to lend a look of quality. Chrome trim and small windows are unusual in modern cars, but are part of a trend for "retro" (old style) designs.

Country: UK
Date: 1999
Size: 4.8 m (15¾ ft) long
Body: steel
Top speed: from 184 km/h
(115 mph) depending on engine
On board: 5

Country: USA
Date: 2000
Size: 4.7 m (15½ ft) long
Body: steel
Top speed: 175 km/h (109 mph)
On board: up to 7

Rover 75

Chrysler Voyager

Chrysler Voyager

As a multi-purpose vehicle, or MPV, the Chrysler *Voyager* was intended to provide the space of a small mini-bus and the comfort of a luxury car. Features include chairs that swivel to face each other and sliding doors on each side to give ease of access.

19

Compact cars

Small cars have small engines, use less fuel and so are cheaper to run. Their size makes them ideal for manoeuvring through busy city traffic and parking in tight spaces. In the 1950s three-wheeled, rear-engined "bubble cars" started the trend, but the arrival of the Fiat *500* and the *Mini* in the late 1950s paved the way for the boom in compact cars. Later models, such as Renault's 5 and *Clio*, and Volkswagen's *Polo* and *Golf* continued the compact cars' popularity.

Citroën 2CV

Citroën 2CV

"Four wheels under an umbrella" was the brief to the designer of the *2CV* in the 1930s. The design also had to stand up to crossing a field without breaking a basket of eggs on board. The *Deux Chevaux* (two horses) or *2CV* had a tiny air-cooled engine, lift-off doors, fold-back roof and removable hammock seats. By 1984, five million had been sold.

Country: France
Date: 1948
Size: from 3.8 m (12½ ft) long
Body: steel
Top speed: from 55 km/h (35 mph)
On board: 4

Heinkel/Trojan 200

Zippy three-wheeler "bubble cars" were produced by famous German aircraft manufacturers such as Messerschmitt and Heinkel. This model was later manufactured in Britain as the *Trojan*. Powered by a small single-cylinder motorcycle engine, it had a single front door but could still house two people in comfort. They continued into the 1960s, until the *Mini* put an end to this particular fashion.

Country: Germany, UK
Date: 1956
Size: 2.4 m (7¾ ft) long
Body: steel
Top speed: 88 km/h (55 mph)
On board: 2

Heinkel/Trojan 200

Austin Seven

One of the most famous cars of all, the *Austin Seven* set a new style for mass motoring during its 16-year life. Sturdier than the fragile cycle-cars of the day, it was very affordable with many versions from tiny two-seaters to graceful saloons.

Austin Seven

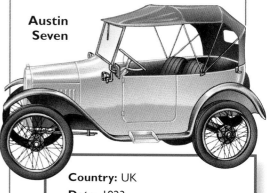

Country: UK
Date: 1923
Size: 2.7 m (8¾ ft) long
Body: steel
Top speed: 64 km/h (40 mph)
On board: 2 to 4 depending on body style

Mini

At a time when most cars had dull designs, Alec Issigonis's *Mini* was revolutionary. This tiny car had good interior space thanks to an engine fitted across the frame driving the front wheels. In its *Mini-Cooper* form, it had great racing success.

Mini

Country: UK
Date: 1959
Size: 3 m (10 ft) long
Body: steel
Top speed: from 115 km/h (72 mph)
On board: 4

Fiat 500

Fiat 500

The *Nuove Cinquecento* or *500* was the first true four-seater mini-car. It replaced the 1930s two-seater *Topolino* ("Little Mouse"), the first car for many Italian families. The 500cc twin-cylinder engine was hidden behind the back seat, so the bonnet was for luggage. By the time this tiny machine gave way to the Fiat *126* in the 1970s over 3 million had been sold.

Country: Italy
Date: 1957
Size: 2.7 m (9 ft) long
Body: steel
Top speed: 96 km/h (60 mph)
On board: 2 to 4

Ford Ka

Country: Europe
Date: 1996
Size: 3.6 m (11¾ ft) long
Body: steel
Top speed: 155 km/h (96 mph)
On board: 4

Ford Ka

Ford's smallest car had a very round body and large plastic mouldings all round to give it an unmistakable design. It came with all kinds of gadgets, such as air conditioning and anti-lock brakes. The *Ka* was selected for exhibition at the New York Museum of Modern Art for its styling and shape.

Toyota Yaris

Toyota's baby hatchback was acclaimed as European Car of the Year 2000. An apparently new concept saw the designers working out what interior space was needed for comfort and then building the car around that. This gave a tall yet compact car, with good seating for four.

Toyota Yaris

Country: Japan
Date: 1999
Size: 3.6 m (11¾ ft) long
Body: steel
Top speed: 154 km/h (96 mph) depending on model
On board: 4

Sports cars

Sports cars are designed to accelerate from 0 to 100 km/h (0–60 mph) in just a few seconds, and some can reach speeds of up to 300 km/h (185 mph). Even though such speeds are well over legal road limits, people love the thrill of handling such powerful machines, especially compared with family saloons which are heavier, slower and less responsive to fast turning or accelerating. Typical sports cars are two-seaters with a soft-top roof that can be folded down.

BMW Z3

Country:
  Germany, USA
Date: 1997
Size: from 4 m (13¼ ft) long
Body: steel
Top speed: up to 224 km/h
  (140 mph)
On board: 2

Country: France
Date: 1997
Size: 3.8 m (12½ ft) long
Body: fibreglass
Top speed: 214 km/h (135 mph)
On board: 2

Renault Spider

The *Spider* is an ultra-light and very basic two-seater, with a fibreglass body and an aluminium chassis. It is unlike anything else that Renault has made. Just behind the seats is the 2.0-litre engine which drives the rear wheels, and gives the *Spider* great stability when cornering.

BMW Z3

Built first in the USA for the Americans, this little German sports car quickly became popular in Europe too. It is a traditional sports car, with only two seats and a front 3.2-litre engine driving the rear wheels. The Z3 also comes with an electrically operated hood.

Porsche 911

Renault Spider

Jaguar XK-SS

This was a road-going version of the Le Mans 24-hour racing cars, the 1950s *D-type* Jaguars. Only 16 cars were completed before fire destroyed the factory where they were built. Those few cars are very valuable today, and the curved design of the *XK-SS* was developed into the world-famous *E-type* Jaguar.

Country: UK
Date: 1957
Size: from 4.3 m (14¼ ft) long
Body: steel
Top speed: 240 km/h (149 mph)
On board: 2

Country: Germany
Date: 1964
Size: from 4.3 m (12¼ ft) long
Body: steel
Top speed: 290 km/h (181 mph)
  in turbo versions
On board: 2

Porsche 911

The *911* was first made in 1964 and continued until 1997 without changing its sleek, aerodynamic shape. All models had their air-cooled engines mounted behind the rear wheels, and they required care when cornering at speed.

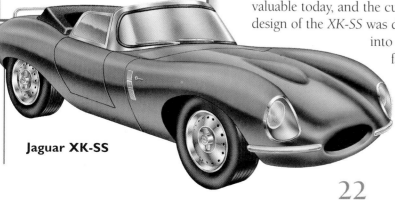
Jaguar XK-SS

Alfa Romeo Montreal

Alfa Romeo Montreal

Italian car-makers Alfa Romeo have produced world-beating racing and touring cars since the 1920s. Named after the Canadian city where it was first shown, the coupé *Montreal* was powered by a version of the V8 engine that was also in Alfa Romeo's successful *Tipo 33* racing cars of the 1960s and 1970s.

Country: Italy
Date: 1970
Size: from 4.2 m (13 ft) long
Body: steel
Top speed: 220 km/h (137 mph)
On board: 2+2

Country: USA
Date: 1953
Size: from 4 m (13 ft) long
Body: fibreglass
Top speed: about 160 km/h (100 mph)
On board: 2

Chevrolet Corvette

Chevrolet Corvette

For many years the *Corvette* was the best known American sports car, and the first to be mass-produced with a fibreglass body. They are still made today but they look nothing like those early models, which have since became highly sought-after collectables.

Aston Martin DBR2

The DB series of Aston Martins were named after David Brown, who once owned the company. The *DBR2* was a very smooth and sleek sports racing car. Its very powerful 3.7-litre engine helped it win the Le Mans 24-hour race and the World Sports Car Championship in 1959.

Aston Martin DBR2

Country: UK
Date: 1957
Size: 4.2 m (13¾ ft) long
Body: steel
Top speed: 280 km/h (175 mph)
On board: 2

Ferrari 250 GTO

Only 39 of the *250 GTOs* were built, and this is one of the most sought-after cars today. Its sleek coupé bodywork was developed after wind tunnel tests at Pisa University which, in the early 1960s, was still unusual. With a mighty V12 engine, the *GTO* could reach over 260 km/h (160 mph).

Country: Italy
Date: 1962
Size: 4.4 m (14½ ft) long
Body: steel
Top speed: 266 km/h (165 mph)
On board: 4

Ferrari 250 GTO

Off-road vehicles

The first off-road car was the General Purpose vehicle, shortened to GP, and nicknamed "Jeep". It became famous during World War II (1939–45) when different models and sizes carried the US army almost anywhere. Its powerful engine, four-wheel drive (previous cars were two-wheel drive only) and large, deep-tread tyres enabled troops to go through desert, ice, mud and other difficult terrain. After the war people began using *Jeeps* and cars like them for fun and exploring. Today's *Jeeps* are much more comfortable with leather-seats and air-conditioning.

Land Rover

Willys Jeep

The *Jeep* was built by a number of companies during World War II to a standard design approved by the US Army, but it was Willys who registered the name in 1945. Very basic, it was also rugged and surprisingly fast. 635,000 examples were made before peace came.

Willys Jeep

Land Rover

With a steel frame and aluminium body panels, early models had three "bucket"-shaped seats up front, and one even featured a central steering wheel. By 1976, one million had been sold worldwide to farmers, the police and the army for working in rough and slippery conditions.

Country: UK
Date: 1948
Size: 4 m (13 ft) long
Body: aluminium alloy
Top speed: 136 km/h (85 mph)
On board: 2 to 9

Country: USA
Date: 1940
Size: 3.3 m (11 ft) long
Body: steel
Top speed: 113 km/h (70 mph)
On board: 4

Country: UK
Date: 1970
Size: 4.5 m (14¾ ft) long
Body: aluminium and steel
Top speed: 160 km/h (100 mph)
On board: 5

Range Rover

Mercedes M Class

The German Mercedes *M Class* is built for the American market. It has leather seats, air conditioning, four airbags and an on-board computer. Special suspension and insulation makes it even more comfortable on rough ground. It can also go through half a metre (2 ft) of water without flooding.

Range Rover

The large and comfortable *Range Rover* was designed as an ATV (all terrain vehicle) to handle normal city streets or difficult muddy forest tracks. With a big V8 engine driving all four wheels it was also powerful, so that it could pull itself up steep hills or through the muddiest country.

Country: Germany, USA
Date: 1998
Size: 4.6 m (15 ft) long
Body: steel
Top speed: 180 km/h (112 mph)
On board: 5 to 7

Mercedes M Class

Jeep Wrangler

Country: USA
Date: 1998
Size: 3.9 m (12¾ ft) long
Body: steel
Top speed: 147 km/h (92 mph)
On board: 4

Jeep Wrangler

This modern open top is fun and safe. It comes equipped with safety features such as airbags, all-steel doors and a skid plate under the fuel tank and a gearbox case to protect the underside of the vehicle. Four-wheel drive can be selected on the move if needed suddenly.

Toyota Land Cruiser

Launched as a basic but rugged all-terrain vehicle, the *Land Cruiser* has sold in vast numbers worldwide. Today, it is made in two luxury versions, the *Colorado* and the *Amazon*. There is an on-board compass, an inclinometer to tell you how steep a track is, and even an altitude display. This is a people carrier with the roadholding stability of a four-wheel drive.

Country: Japan
Date: 2000
Size: 4.3 m (14 ft) long
Body: steel
Top speed: 160 km/h (100 mph)
On board: 8

Toyota Land Cruiser

Country: USA
Date: 2000
Size: 4.8 m (15¾ ft) long
Body: steel
Top speed: 160 km/h (100 mph)
On board: 5

Ford Explorer

An old favourite in the USA, the *Explorer* was not introduced to Europe until 1997, but it is now a top-selling off-road vehicle. It features a big engine, selectable four-wheel drive and automatic transmission (clutch and gearbox) to help it through tough terrain. It is also well equipped for family motoring. Air conditioning, electric windows, mirrors, sliding roof and seats, cruise control and even an electronic compass are some of the on-board items.

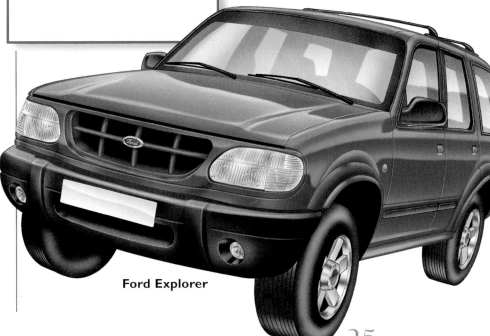

Ford Explorer

25

The race flags

Officials at race meetings still use flags to get messages to drivers, though most communications are electronic and the cars have radios.

 Yellow flag shows that there is danger ahead, such as an accident.

 Blue flag shows that a faster car is coming up, usually to lap a driver.

 Green flag shows that the track is clear, particularly after yellow flags.

 Black flag with a car's number on it indicates that the car must stop.

 Red flag shows that a race has been stopped.

 White flag warns there is a slow moving vehicle ahead (ie. an ambulance).

 Yellow and red flag warns that the track ahead is unusually slippery.

 Chequered flag is waved at the finish line. when the winner passes.

Crash helmet

Flameproof protection suit

Formula One cars

Formula One cars are the fastest – reaching speeds of 320 km/h (200 mph) – and the drivers are the most skilled in the world. There is only room for one person, who sits in front of the engine. The wheels are uncovered and the tyres are very wide to grip the road well. Wings are used at the front and back to press the cars down and help them to go around corners fast. The wings give so much downwards force at high speed that the cars could drive along a ceiling upside down without falling off.

The pit crew

A large team of people look after each car at a Grand Prix race. They work very fast during the race, changing four tyres and filling the fuel tank in less than 10 seconds.

Protective clothing

Every driver wears a crash helmet to protect his head in a crash and a special suit to help prevent injury if a fire starts after an accident. The suit is made of several layers of special fireproof fabric.

Front wing or aerofoil

F1 CAR DESIGN

26

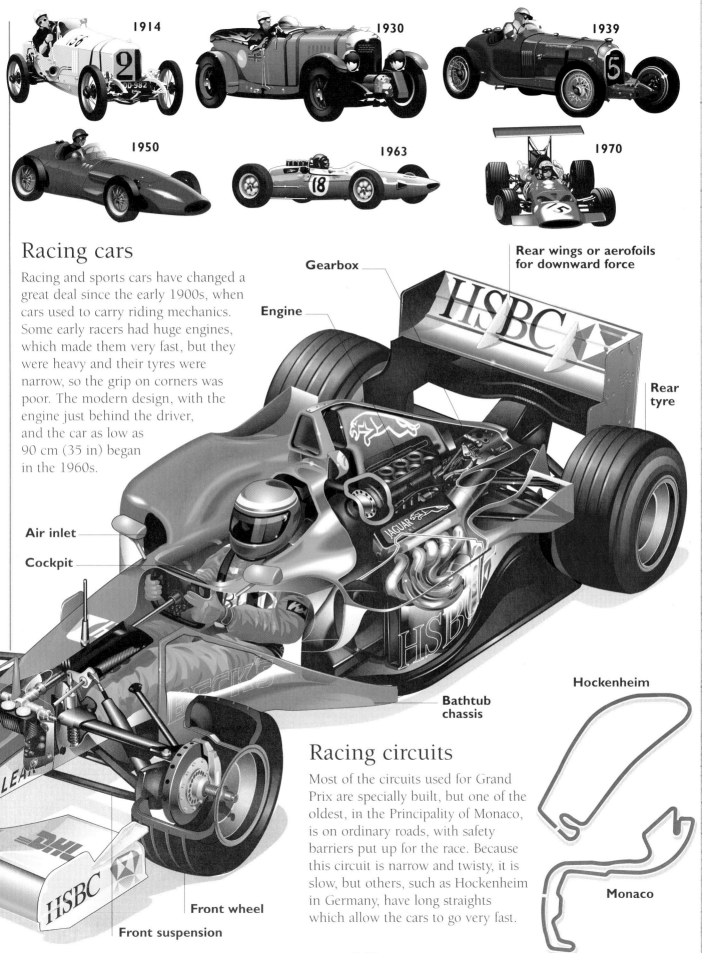

1914

1930

1939

1950

1963

1970

Racing cars

Racing and sports cars have changed a great deal since the early 1900s, when cars used to carry riding mechanics. Some early racers had huge engines, which made them very fast, but they were heavy and their tyres were narrow, so the grip on corners was poor. The modern design, with the engine just behind the driver, and the car as low as 90 cm (35 in) began in the 1960s.

Gearbox

Engine

Rear wings or aerofoils for downward force

Rear tyre

Air inlet

Cockpit

Bathtub chassis

Front wheel

Front suspension

Racing circuits

Most of the circuits used for Grand Prix are specially built, but one of the oldest, in the Principality of Monaco, is on ordinary roads, with safety barriers put up for the race. Because this circuit is narrow and twisty, it is slow, but others, such as Hockenheim in Germany, have long straights which allow the cars to go very fast.

Hockenheim

Monaco

Autosports

Since the earliest days of motoring there have been motor races: the French Grand Prix dates back to 1906. At that time racing cars were huge machines capable of 145 km/h (90 mph). Today's race cars can comfortably reach 320 km/h (200 mph). But not all racing takes place on a race track. Rallying is almost like off-road racing, often on dirt tracks, where the driver relies on sideway spins to corner, the opposite of circuit racing, in which smooth turning drivers are the quickest.

Country: various
Date: 1992
Size: 1.8 m (6 ft) long
Body: steel tube frame and seat
Top speed: 240 km/h (150 mph)
On board: 2

Ford Focus

Ford Focus

This rally version of a standard *Focus* has extra body strength and special suspension. The engine produces more than twice as much power as the standard road car, so it can go at very high speeds on rough windy tracks, often through thick forests. When they are rallying, the driver and his navigator talk to each other through an intercom in their helmets because it is so noisy.

Zip Kart

This kart is light enough to be picked up by one person. It is made up of a tube frame with a seat, a steering wheel, pedals and a small engine at the back. Because it is so small, it can "zip" round Grand Prix circuits at 240 km/h (150 mph), and its tiny tyres are wide enough to allow the kart to go round corners very fast. Less powerful 40-km/h (25-mph) versions are popular at go-kart tracks.

Country: UK
Date: 2000
Size: 4.2 m (13¼ ft) long
Body: reinforced steel and carbon fibre
Top speed: 240 km/h (150 mph)
On board: 2

Country: France
Date: 1999
Size: 4.6 m (15 ft) long
Body: steel and composites
Top speed: 180 km/h (112 mph)
On board: 2

Schlesser Renault Buggy

Jean-Louis Schlesser's *Buggy* is strengthened and has special springs to tackle the tough desert surfaces on the 10,000 km (6,250 miles) Paris-Dakar Rally (Europe to Africa). The engine is from a Renault *Megane* road car, but it is highly modified for extra power.

Schlesser Renault Buggy

Audi/Le Mans

Audis are not usually associated with the famous Le Mans 24-hour race, but in 2000 an aerodynamic racing *Audi* won the event. It is built of lightweight materials, such as carbon fibre, and its engine, which sits behind the driver can power it to speeds of well over 300 km/h (185 mph).

Daf SRT-II

A turbo-charged engine helps this racing truck accelerate fast enough to leave most sports cars behind. The cab is strengthened, leaving room for only a driver, and the truck is so light that more weight has to be put on to load it down.

Daf SRT-II

Country: Netherlands
Date: 1998
Size: 4.5 m (14¾ ft)
Body: steel and lightweight composites
Top speed: 180 km/h (112 mph)
On board: 1

Audi/Le Mans

Country: Germany
Date: 2000
Size: 4.6 m (15 ft) long
Body: carbon fibre
Top speed: 320 km/h (200 mph)
On board: 1 (officially 2)

Ford Taurus

This Ford won the 1999 Daytona 500, which is the most famous NASCAR (National Association for Stock Car Auto Racing) event. It looks like a standard "stock" or saloon car that customers can buy, but in fact it has been altered to speed along banked oval circuits in some 30 US races each year.

Country: USA
Date: 1999
Size: 5 m (16 ft) long
Body: lightweight alloys
Top speed: 340 km/h (200 mph)
On board: 1

Ford Taurus

Reynard 961

Country: USA
Date: 1996
Size: 5 m (16 ft) long
Body: lightweight composites
Top speed: 376 km/h (335 mph)
On board: 1

Reynard 961

Like many Indy cars racing on the American road and oval race circuits, the Reynard is built in the UK. Though they look like Formula One racers (see pages 26–27), average lap speeds of these US racing cars are 373 km/h (232 mph), and they run on alcohol fuel not petrol. A gear change takes 16 milliseconds, and a gearbox copes in two hours with what a road car suffers in a lifetime.

War-zone vehicles

The first military vehicles were the wheeled siege towers and battering rams used by the Assyrians of Asia in the 9th century BC. Leonardo da Vinci drew a battle car in 1484, and in 1855 James Cowen invented an armed, wheeled, armoured vehicle based on the steam tractor. World War I (1914–18), saw real mechanised warfare with the first steel-plated tanks. They moved on metal chains called tracks, and today are armed with powerful cannons on revolving turrets.

AC armoured car

Country: UK
Date: 1916
Size: 8.1 m (26½ ft) long
Body: armoured steel plates
Top speed: 6 km/h (3¾ mph)
On board: 8

AC armoured car

This gunless armoured car, made by AC, was one of the first produced. It had an ordinary car frame, with thick steel body work to protect the crew. The driver looked ahead through a small slit in the front and even the radiator had armoured doors. However, the wheels could easily be damaged and the tyres punctured in action.

Country: UK
Date: 1914
Size: 3.7 m (12 ft) long
Body: heavy steel
Top speed: 50 km/h (31 mph)
On board: 6

Vickers tank

Tanks were first made with caterpillar tracks to cross mud, trenches and barbed wire during World War I. They were called "tanks" to conceal their real purpose from the enemy. The "male" *Vickers* had cannons on the side and the "female" had machine guns. Their first battle was the Somme in 1916. Inside they were very hot, noisy and uncomfortable.

DUKW

DUKWs were nicknamed "Ducks" because they could travel over water from ship to shore at 10 km/h (6¼ mph). All the wheels steered, and helped the rudder in water. About 1,000 *DUKWs* took part in the invasion of Sicily (1943).

Country: Germany
Date: 1940
Size: 3.8 m (12½ ft) long
Body: steel
Top speed: 90 km/h (56 mph)
On board: 4

DUKW

Kubelwagen

Kubelwagen

The *Kubelwagen* was the German army's version of the VW *Beetle* (see page 18). It was designed by Dr Porsche and during World War II (1939–45) more than 50,000 were built. It did not have four-wheel drive, like the *Jeep* (see page 24), but with very simple mechanical parts, it was reliable. It was used to carry soldiers in battle areas, and there was even an amphibious version called the *Schwimmwagen*.

Country: USA
Date: 1943
Size: 6 m (20 ft) long
Body: mainly steel
Top speed: 80 km/h
   (50 mph) on land
On board: 25 to 30

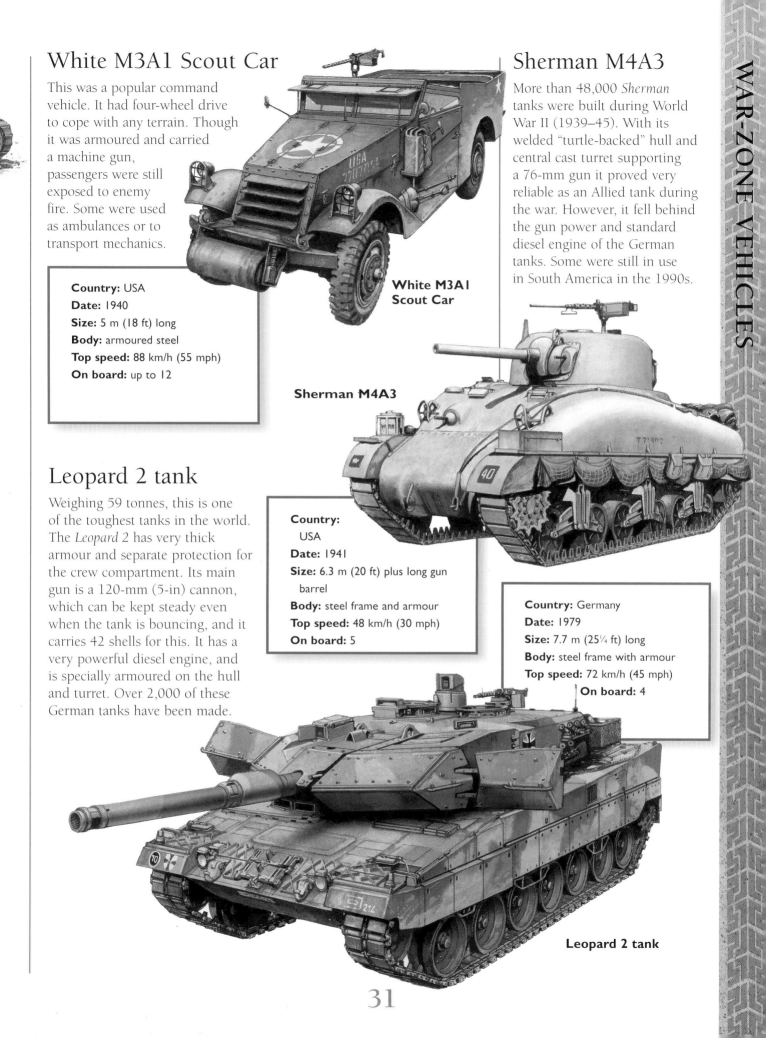

White M3A1 Scout Car

This was a popular command vehicle. It had four-wheel drive to cope with any terrain. Though it was armoured and carried a machine gun, passengers were still exposed to enemy fire. Some were used as ambulances or to transport mechanics.

White M3A1 Scout Car

Country: USA
Date: 1940
Size: 5 m (18 ft) long
Body: armoured steel
Top speed: 88 km/h (55 mph)
On board: up to 12

Sherman M4A3

More than 48,000 *Sherman* tanks were built during World War II (1939–45). With its welded "turtle-backed" hull and central cast turret supporting a 76-mm gun it proved very reliable as an Allied tank during the war. However, it fell behind the gun power and standard diesel engine of the German tanks. Some were still in use in South America in the 1990s.

Sherman M4A3

Country: USA
Date: 1941
Size: 6.3 m (20 ft) plus long gun barrel
Body: steel frame and armour
Top speed: 48 km/h (30 mph)
On board: 5

Leopard 2 tank

Weighing 59 tonnes, this is one of the toughest tanks in the world. The *Leopard 2* has very thick armour and separate protection for the crew compartment. Its main gun is a 120-mm (5-in) cannon, which can be kept steady even when the tank is bouncing, and it carries 42 shells for this. It has a very powerful diesel engine, and is specially armoured on the hull and turret. Over 2,000 of these German tanks have been made.

Country: Germany
Date: 1979
Size: 7.7 m (25¼ ft) long
Body: steel frame with armour
Top speed: 72 km/h (45 mph)
On board: 4

Leopard 2 tank

Emergency vehicles

We often see brightly-marked police cars, ambulances, pick-up trucks, recovery vans and fire engines with lights flashing or sirens wailing, hurrying through traffic. So it is hard to imagine that the earliest ambulances and fire engines were pulled by horses or people. A modern fire truck can carry 4,500 litres (1,000 gallons) of water through 450 m (1,500 ft) of hose.

Willeme 5471

This aircraft recovery truck was built on a standard Willeme chassis (frame), but was specially adapted to recover aircraft that had broken down. It had 12 wheels on four axles so that it could carry loads of up to 150 tonnes. A massive crane on the back was used to lift the aircraft, and the front of the truck had to be very heavy to make sure that it did not tip up.

Country: France
Date: 1956
Size: 10.7 m (35 ft) long
Body: steel frame and cab
Top speed: 60 km/h (37½ mph)
On board: 2

Willeme 5471

Merryweather fire appliance

This fire engine had one of the early turntable ladders, which could be raised automatically to reach tall buildings quickly. The pump was driven by the truck's engine and could push water through its hoses up to a height of 40 m (130 ft).

Merryweather fire appliance

Country: UK
Date: 1922
Size: 7.4 m (24¼ ft) long, plus ladder
Body: steel frame and cab
Top speed: 56 km/h (35 mph)
On board: 4

Country: USA
Date: 1989
Size: approx. 48 m (158 ft) long
Body: steel and aluminium
Top speed: 65 km/h (105 mph)
On board: 6

US fire truck

This truck is very big and it has all kinds of equipment on board. Its ladder has a platform on its top and can go as high as a seven-storey building. It can also rotate 360° and the platform has two water cannons which can squirt about 5,600 litres (1,222 gallons) of water a minute on to a fire. Outrigger legs on the side of the truck keep it steady when the platform is being used and the truck has many spotlights and floodlights.

NYPD Impala

Country: USA
Date: 2000
Size: 5.1 m (16¾ ft) long
Body: steel
Top speed: 198 km/h (124 mph)
On board: 6

NYPD Impala

The NYPD (New York Police Department) version of the Chevrolet *Impala* has a lot of special equipment. The engine is bigger and more powerful, the brakes are large and the springs are tough. The roof lights and siren make sure that people know the police are coming. On the front are push bars that let the police move or stop other cars without damage.

Country: Yugoslavia
Date: 1975
Size: 6.2 m (20¼ ft) long
Body: armoured steel and glass
Top speed: possibly 90 km/h (55 mph)
On board: possibly 2 to 4

FAP riot control

Specially designed to deal with rioting crowds, this van has four-wheel drive for rough or slippery ground and extremely tough bodywork. The exposed glass is armoured and the headlamps have grills over them. What looks like a gun on the top is a water cannon, powerful enough to knock over and push back rioters. It is supplied from a big tank inside the van.

FAP riot control

US fire truck

US wrecker

This piece of equipment took well over a year to complete and is designed for towing and heavy duty recovery. The truck was made separately from the wrecker body. The wrecker body was built in Texas and mounted onto the stretched out frame of the truck which came from another part of the USA.

Country: USA
Date: 1997
Size: 12 m (39½ ft) long
Body: steel
Top speed: approx. 90 km/h (56 mph)
On board: 1, sometimes 2

US wrecker

Trucks

The earliest trucks used petrol engines or steam power, but in the 1920s the German Benz Company introduced diesel-powered trucks. Diesel engines were more powerful and enabled trucks to travel further on a single tank of fuel. Modern trucks are either "rigid" (having a single and straight chassis frame), or "articulated" (jointed) with two parts, a tractor unit which carries the engine, cab and driving wheels, and a detachable trailer.

De Dion Bouton

Vabis 1½-tonne truck

Vabis 1½-tonne truck

One of the first Swedish trucks, this *Vabis* had a simple platform on a steel girder frame. The tiny engine at the front drove the back wheels. There were springs, but the ride was not comfortable for the exposed driver.

Country: Sweden
Date: 1903
Size: 4½ m (15 ft) long
Body: wood and steel with wooden wheels and steel tyres
Top speed: 20 km/h (12½ mph)
On board: 2

De Dion Bouton

Even in the early 1920s, some trucks were purpose-built to perform special tasks. This *De Dion Bouton* road-sweeper had a brush that turned as the truck moved and collected roadside rubbish. The dirt was then sucked into the bag on the back of the truck. The rest of the truck was old-fashioned with open cabin sides and cart-type wheels.

Country: France
Date: 1922
Size: 5 m (16½ ft) long
Body: wood and steel
Top speed: 32 km/h (20 mph)
On board: 2

CAT 621E scraper

These huge machines are often seen alongside new big roads being built. Even the tyres are taller than a person. These machines can scrape up to 33 cm (13 in) of earth at a time to level the surface, and carry nearly 22 tonnes of soil. The scraper is on a swivelling link to the tractor at the front, and both parts have a powerful diesel engine.

Scammel Scarab

The *Scarab* could turn round in small spaces, because of a clever pivot between the cab and the trailer, the pointed nose and the single front wheel. It was ideal for stations, where one tractor could handle several trailers.

Country: UK
Date: 1949
Size: 9 m (29½ ft) long
Body: steel (later fibreglass cab)
Top speed: 48 km/h (30 mph)
On board: 2

Scammel Scarab

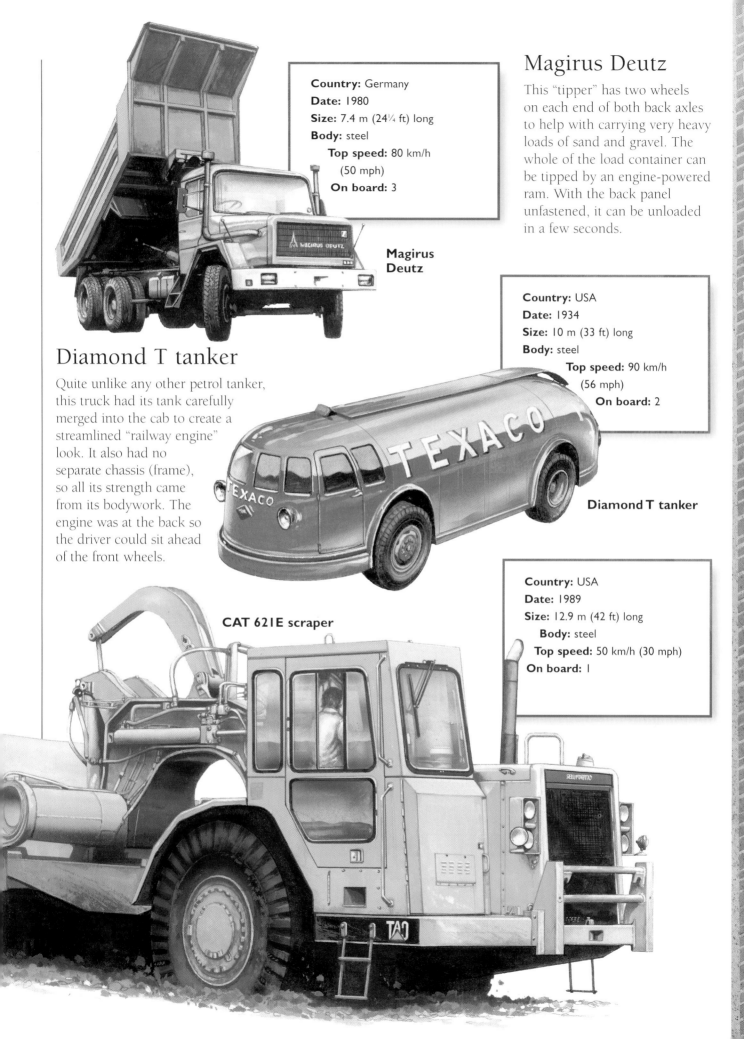

Magirus Deutz

This "tipper" has two wheels on each end of both back axles to help with carrying very heavy loads of sand and gravel. The whole of the load container can be tipped by an engine-powered ram. With the back panel unfastened, it can be unloaded in a few seconds.

Country: Germany
Date: 1980
Size: 7.4 m (24¼ ft) long
Body: steel
Top speed: 80 km/h (50 mph)
On board: 3

Magirus Deutz

Diamond T tanker

Quite unlike any other petrol tanker, this truck had its tank carefully merged into the cab to create a streamlined "railway engine" look. It also had no separate chassis (frame), so all its strength came from its bodywork. The engine was at the back so the driver could sit ahead of the front wheels.

Country: USA
Date: 1934
Size: 10 m (33 ft) long
Body: steel
Top speed: 90 km/h (56 mph)
On board: 2

Diamond T tanker

CAT 621E scraper

Country: USA
Date: 1989
Size: 12.9 m (42 ft) long
Body: steel
Top speed: 50 km/h (30 mph)
On board: 1

Buses

Some of the earliest buses were double-decker horse-drawn trams which ran through the streets on rails (see page 94). Motor-powered buses and trolleys appeared in the early 1900s. Most buses today run on their own engines, while trolley buses are powered by electricity from overhead cables. Long-distance buses come with individual lighting, air controls and reclining seats, and are equipped with toilets.

(see page 94)

Germain open top

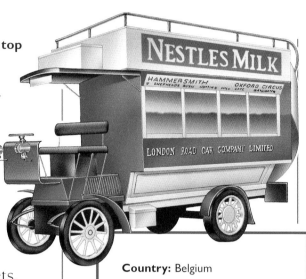

Country: Belgium
Date: 1904
Size: 7 m (24 ft) long
Body: wood and steel
Top speed: 32 km/h (20 mph)
On board: 32

Bean single deck

Country: UK
Date: 1930
Size: 6 m (19½ ft) long
Body: aluminium and wood
Top speed: 75 km/h (46¾ mph)
On board: 18

Bean single deck

By today's standards the *Bean*'s engine was not powerful, and it took up a lot of room. With the driver and the door behind him, there was even less room for passengers. If the engine stopped, the driver might have to resort to re-starting the bus by winding the handle hanging from the front.

Germain open top

Early buses, like this *Germain*, were built on a lorry chassis. This one, which was used in London, had its driver sitting on the bonnet to leave as much room as possible for passengers. An outside staircase led to the roof. People would have a good view from there, but would get wet if it rained. The ride was slow and bumpy and the buses often broke down.

Sunbeam trolley bus

Trolley buses have electric motors. They pick up electricity through "trollers" (arms) on the roof that run along overhead wires. They do not run on rails as trams do. On this double-decker version, the stairs to the top deck were at the back and a conductor collected the fares while on the move. Sometimes, the arms would come off the wires and the driver would use a special long pole to push them back up.

Country: UK
Date: 1946
Size: 10 m (32¾ ft) long
Body: steel
Top speed: 64 km/h (40 mph)
On board: 66

Sunbeam trolley bus

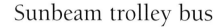

MCI courier

Berliet PCM bus

Berliet PCM bus

Although this French bus looks modern, it is more than 30 years old. It has doors at the front and the back, operated by the driver, so that passengers can enter and leave without crowding. There is plenty of room for standing as well as sitting, with handrails to hold on to. The layout in which the driver sits alongside the engine is called forward control.

Country: France
Date: 1968
Size: 10 m (32¾ ft) long
Body: steel and fibreglass
Top speed: 100 km/h (62 mph)
On board: 40

AmTran school bus

American school buses are made by many different companies, but they are always yellow and easy to spot. This one has a high floor with low doors for ease of access. Multiple mirrors allow the driver to make sure it is safe to drive off, and flashing lights on the top warn other motorists.

AmTran school bus

Country: USA
Date: 1999
Size: 9.5 m (31¼ ft) long
Body: welded steel
Top speed: 105 km/h (65 mph)
On board: 54

Country: USA, Canada
Date: 1948
Size: 10.5 m (34½ ft) long
Body: wood and steel
Top speed: 85 km/h (53 mph)
On board: 33

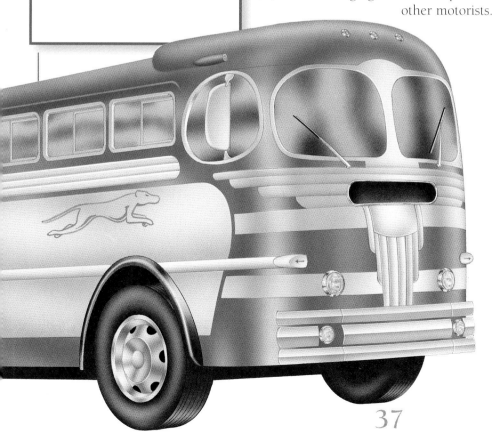

MCI courier

This single-decker was the standard inter-city passenger bus in the USA and Canada in the late 1940s and early 1950s. The American Greyhound line covers vast distances, so comfort is important. This was one of the first buses to have reclining seats. The high floor meant that passengers had a good view and that luggage could be stowed in a compartment below.

37

Pedal power

Most modern bicycles are still based on designs over 150 years old. The first pedal cycle was the *velocipe* of 1865, built by Michaux in France. It was very heavy and the thick iron tyres made the ride very bumpy, leading to the nickname "boneshaker". Today, some bikes are so light they can be lifted with just a finger. HPV (human powered vehicles) are also pedal-powered, but the rider reclines in a bucket seat and steers with a joystick.

Penny-farthing

Dandy horse

Country: France
Date: 1816
Size: 1.8 m (6 ft)
Body: iron frame and wheels, with leather saddle
Propulsion: feet on ground

Dandy horse

Also called the "hobby horse", this bicycle had two spoked wheels in line joined by a frame, just like a modern bike, but it had no pedals. Instead, the rider walked while sitting astride the machine to speeds of 15 km/h (9½ mph).

Country: UK, USA, France
Date: 1872
Size: 1.5 m (5 ft)
Body: steel frame and spoked wheels, with leather saddle
Propulsion: pedals on front wheel

Penny-farthing

The earliest bicycles had the pedals working directly on the front wheels. This meant that a bigger wheel made the bike travel further for each turn, so the wheels grew bigger (and the back wheel smaller) until some were 1.5 m (5 ft) across. This was the ordinary bicycle of 1872, better known as the *penny-farthing* because it resembled two coins of the day.

Country: UK
Date: 1886
Size: 1.7 m (5¾ ft)
Body: tubular steel frame with rubber tyres and leather saddle
Propulsion: chain drive from pedals

Starley's Safety 1886

Raleigh Superbe

Touring bikes such as the *Raleigh Superbe* were made in the 1950s as the demand for cycles for leisure travellers and commuters increased. Its simple three-speed gear system made climbing hills easier, the chain had a cover to keep grease off clothes and there were mudguards and lights.

Raleigh Superbe

Country: UK
Date: 1949
Size: 1.8 m (6 ft)
Body: tubular steel frame with leather saddle and steel mudguards
Propulsion: chain drive from pedals, with gears

Starley's Safety 1886

This bicycle looked very much like a modern bicycle with equal-sized wheels. It featured a rear wheel driven by a large chain wheel on the pedals, and a small chain wheel on the rear wheel giving it gears. The tyres were solid rubber and the bike shook a lot, but it made cycling much more popular, taking the place of the *penny-farthing*.

Marin Mount Vision

Country: USA	
Date: 1999	
Size: 1.6 m (5½ ft)	
Body: lightweight aluminium frame with full suspension	
Propulsion: chain drive with 21 gears	

Marin Mount Vision

This lightweight mountain bike was the first with suspension on both front and rear wheels to win a major cross-country championship. The nobbly tyres are tough and give extra grip on loose surfaces. The bike's tubing is made of aircraft-quality aluminium.

GTRZ 1000 Racer

Racing bikes have dropped handlebars so the rider can bend down for low wind resistance. They have thin, high pressured tyres and "derailleur" gears using a tight chain that can be moved from one size of sprocket (small, toothed wheel) to another, either at the pedals or at the wheel. Together there can be as many as 21 gears.

Country: UK	
Date: 1992	
Size: 1.8 m (6 ft)	
Body: lightweight carbon composite frame and wheels	
Propulsion: chain drive, no gears	

GTZR 1000 Racer

Country: USA	
Date: 1999	
Size: 1.8 m (6 ft)	
Body: lightweight aluminium frame with carbon fibre forks	
Propulsion: chain drive from pedals with 18 gears	

Lotus Sport bike

Lotus Sport bike

Better known for its sports cars, Lotus came up with a very different looking racing bike in 1992. Chris Boardman of Britain rode one to win a gold medal at the Barcelona Olympics. Instead of traditional steel tubing welded together, this bike was moulded using stronger and lighter carbon fibre composite. New "tri-bar" handlebar designs gave the rider an ultra-low position.

Motorcycles

Motorcycles are two-wheeled vehicles with engines, which a driver straddles as if on a bicycle. Some have a sidecar attached on a third wheel. Mopeds are low-powered motorcycles fitted with pedals to power the engine. Motorcycles also compete in road and cross-country (motocross) racing.

Daimler Einspur

Country: Germany
Date: 1885
Size: 1.5 m (5 ft)
Body: wood and steel
Engine capacity: 264 cc
Speed: under 16 km/h (10 mph)

Henderson 7hp

Henderson 7hp

American motorcycles developed as powerful tourers for the big roads there. This model featured a powerful four-cylinder engine which was unusual for the time, in a very long frame. The machine was hard to control in tight turns. On the highway however, it could cruise at over 80 km/h (50 mph).

Country: USA
Date: 1913
Size: 1.8 m (5¾ ft)
Body: steel
Engine capacity: 1301 cc
Speed: 88 km/h (55 mph)

Daimler Einspur

The Daimler *Einspur* ("single track") may be the first true motorcycle, even though it had extra wheels to keep it stable and a saddle that looked as if it had just been taken off a horse. A tall single-cylinder petrol engine produced just half a horsepower.

Country: USA
Date: 1965
Size: 2m (6½ ft)
Body: steel
Engine capacity: 1207 cc
Speed: 153 km/h (95 mph)

Electra-Glide

Harley-Davidson was founded in 1903. The most famous model the company has ever produced is the 1960s *Electra-Glide* which is still in production, little altered from the original. It is popular with many police forces. The heart of the Glide is a big V-twin engine that produces a distinctive "potato-potato" noise.

Electra-Glide

Country: Italy
Date: 1963
Size: 1.7 m (5½ ft)
Body: steel frame and panels
Engine capacity: 159 cc
Speed: 96 km/h (60 mph)

Vespa GS1 60

Vespa GS1 60

The *Vespa* (Italian for wasp) is a scooter – a motorcycle with a little engine mounted around the back wheel so that the rider sits upright with feet together on a platform. It has a "step-through" frame, most controls (except the rear brake) sited on the handlebars and a powerful enough engine to allow it to zip in and out of traffic.

Honda CB750

With a quiet and revolutionary four-cylinder engine (other bikes had just one or two cylinders) this was the first long-distance touring superbike. When bikes were still thought of as oily and unreliable, the electric-start engine was said to be "sewing-machine-smooth".

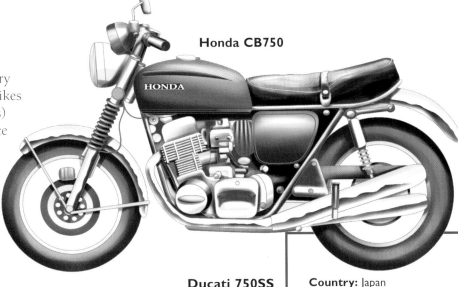

Honda CB750

Ducati 750SS

Country: Japan
Date: 1969
Size: 2 m (6½ ft)
Body: steel
Engine capacity: 736 cc
Speed: 193 km/h (120 mph)

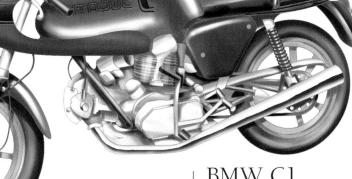

Country: Italy
Date: 1972
Size: 2.1 m (7 ft)
Body: steel
Engine capacity: 748 cc
Speed: 203 km/h (126 mph)

BMW C1

BMW C1

Perhaps the ultimate commuter vehicle, the BMW *C1* runs like a scooter (low-powered engine and low-slung frame with two small wheels). However, a roof, a windscreen (and wiper), side protection bars and twin seat belts have been added for extra safety.

Ducati 750SS

Capable of going over 200 km/h (124 mph), this *Ducati* model was a racing motorcycle for the road. It was also the forerunner of the famous red racers that dominated superbike racing in the 1990s. It had few comforts or frills for the road traveller, and was much more at home screeching at high speed on the race tracks. Its engine was powerful, but the *Ducati* was also renowned for its fine handling and roadholding.

Country: Germany
Date: 2000
Size: 2 m (6½ ft)
Body: aluminium frame, plastic body
Engine capacity: 125 cc
Speed: 100 km/h (62 mph)

Who invented the wheel?

The first wheels were made in about 3500 BC in Mesopotamia, the area between the Tigris and Euphrates rivers, in what is now Iraq. No one knows the names of the craftsmen who made these early wheels, but they probably got the idea from potters, who were using spinning wheels to make vessels out of clay. Like the potters' wheels, these early cartwheels were made out of solid wood. Some 2,000 years later, fast two-wheeled chariots ran on spoked wheels. After another 2,000 years there were metal wheels, improved wheel bearings and air-filled tyres for a bump-free ride.

Tyres were first fitted to wheels by the ancient Egyptians, who covered the rims of their wooden wheels with leather to protect them from wear. Solid rubber tyres appeared in the 1840s, and in 1888 **John Boyd Dunlop** (*shown here*) fitted his son's bicycle with inflatable rubber tyres. Today, most road vehicles have inflatable tyres.

Primitive wheels were made of planks of wood held together with wooden pegs and mounted on axles. These **solid wheels** were used on carts to carry peat and on primitive chariots (*below*), and were very heavy to pull. Craftsmen from Mesopotamia (now in modern Iraq) removed some of the wood to make a wheel with two large holes, the forerunner of the spoked wheel.

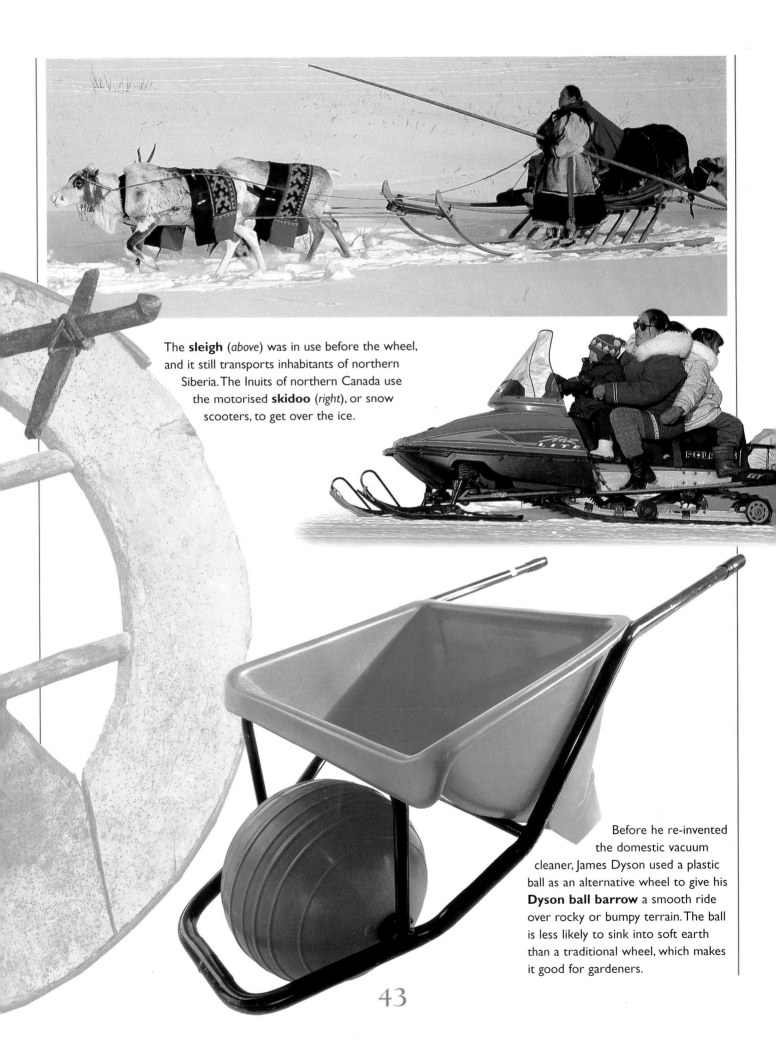

The **sleigh** (*above*) was in use before the wheel, and it still transports inhabitants of northern Siberia. The Inuits of northern Canada use the motorised **skidoo** (*right*), or snow scooters, to get over the ice.

Before he re-invented the domestic vacuum cleaner, James Dyson used a plastic ball as an alternative wheel to give his **Dyson ball barrow** a smooth ride over rocky or bumpy terrain. The ball is less likely to sink into soft earth than a traditional wheel, which makes it good for gardeners.

On water

Boats and ships are the most varied of all forms of transport, ranging from tiny dinghies only a few metres long to vast supertankers that take more than five minutes to walk along. From warships to windsurfers, there are vessels for virtually any task.

In the Stone Age, the earliest boat was a canoe hollowed out of a log. Then came oars and sails followed by steam and petrol engines. Today, wave-piercing water jets and solar-power can propel ships – and the water speed record is now a staggering 511 km/h (317 mph).

Luxury liners (*left*) take holidaying passengers to exotic ports around the world. Such vessels have never been more popular. Cunard's *Queen Mary 2*, for example, being launched in 2003 will carry 2,800 passengers at 55 km/h (34 mph), driven by environmentally friendly gas/turbine diesel power. It will be five times longer than Cunard's first steam ship *Britannia* (see page 57).

Dragonfly

Square sail

Lateen sail

Settee sail

Gaff sail

Lug sail

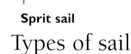

Sprit sail

What is a ship?

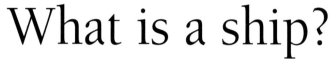

Any large vessel that floats on the water can be called a ship. Smaller craft are called boats, and sailors often say that if a vessel is big enough to carry a boat, then that vessel is a ship. Every ship has a body called a hull, which in ancient times was made of wood but is now more likely to be metal. Ships also have some means of propulsion, such as sails or an engine. They have been around for well over 10,000 years, and are used as warships, pleasure craft and to carry cargo or passengers.

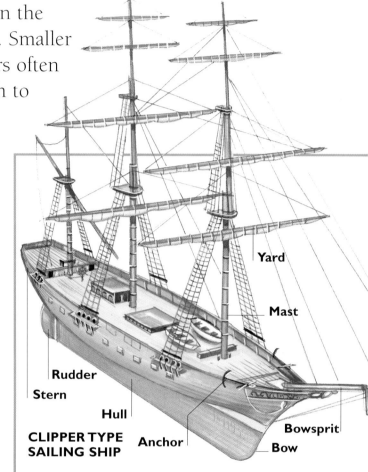

Yard

Mast

Rudder

Stern

Hull

Bowsprit

CLIPPER TYPE SAILING SHIP

Anchor

Bow

Types of sail

There are dozens of types of sail. Western ocean-going ships most commonly used square sails which, in a fully rigged ship could set three or more to a mast. Triangular sails, such as lateen sails or settees, are still favoured in the Arab world.

Parts of a sailing ship

There are several vertical masts, with other timbers, such as horizontal yards, to support the sails. The bow (front) is often pointed, to cut smoothly through the water; the rudder which is used for steering, is at the stern (rear).

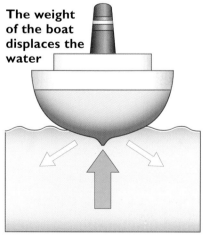

The weight of the boat displaces the water

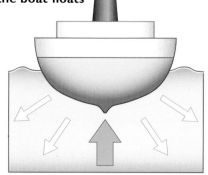

The displaced water now equals the weight of the boat and the boat floats

How a ship floats

A solid object sinks because it weighs more than the amount of water it displaces. All ships are hollow and therefore very light for their size. They only settle into the water until the amount that they displace equals their own total weight. The pressure of the water from below then supports the rest of the ship above the surface.

Propulsion

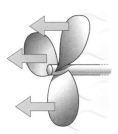

Ships used to have sails or oars, but modern ships usually have an engine. This drives a number of propellers, which push the craft through the water. The first propellers had twin blades, but three- or four-bladed propellers are more efficient and powerful.

Hovercraft

Instead of floating, a hovercraft hovers on a cushion of air just above the surface of the water, or a swamp (or dry land). It has huge fans to create the air cushion, which is held in place by a rubber membrane, called a skirt. This stretches all around the hull.

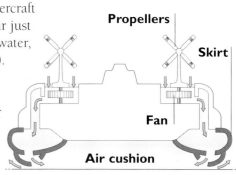

Hydrofoils

One thing that slows ships down is the force, called drag, created by the hull in the water. Hydrofoils get around this problem by raising their hull out of the water on special struts, called foils. Hydrofoils sit in the water like normal craft, but as they gather speed, the foils come into play, lifting up the hulls. This means that these craft can go much faster than standard vessels of the same power.

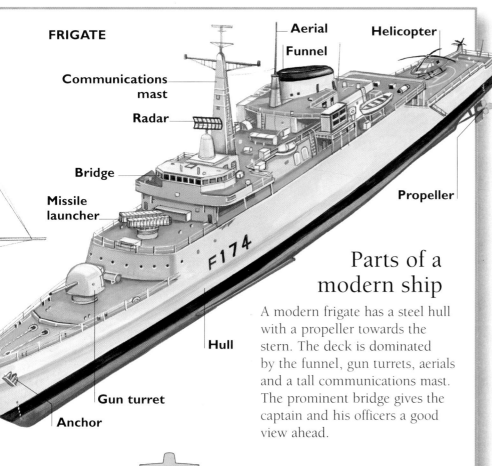

FRIGATE

- Aerial
- Funnel
- Helicopter
- Communications mast
- Radar
- Bridge
- Missile launcher
- Propeller
- F174
- Hull
- Gun turret
- Anchor

Parts of a modern ship

A modern frigate has a steel hull with a propeller towards the stern. The deck is dominated by the funnel, gun turrets, aerials and a tall communications mast. The prominent bridge gives the captain and his officers a good view ahead.

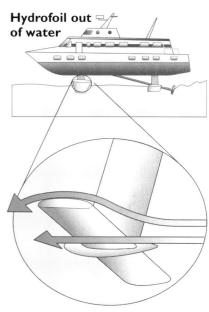

At speed the foil lifts the hull out of the water

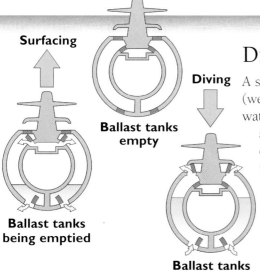

Surfacing

Diving

Ballast tanks empty

Ballast tanks being emptied

Ballast tanks filling up

Diving a submarine

A submarine contains large ballast (weight) tanks (heavily weighted with water): these can be filled or emptied as the vessel moves. When the captain wants to dive, he orders the tanks to be filled with water. This increases the weight and density of the submarine, which makes the vessel sink. To rise back to the surface, the water is pumped out from the tanks.

47

Venturing onto water

Many of the first boats, including the North American kayak and the Polynesian outrigger, were so well crafted that similar boats are still used to transport people and goods 5,000 years later. When people first began to build boats, some chopped down tree trunks to make rafts or canoes, while others chose thin branches and animal skins to make frame boats. Ancient sailing vessels like dhows and junks are still made today and sail in the Arabian and China seas.

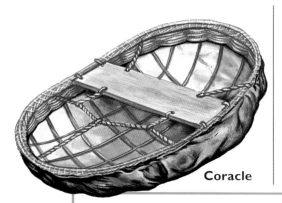
Coracle

Country: Ireland, Wales
Date: from pre-history
Size: 2 m (6½ ft) long
Construction: hide on wicker framework
Speed: about 6 km/h (3½ mph)
On board: 1

Dugout canoe

Dugout canoe

The canoe was probably the first type of boat to be made. It consists of a tree trunk shaped and hollowed out in the middle to make a place where people could sit and paddle. Early people used simple stone axes to carve the wood to get the best hull shape. They used fire to hollow out the middle.

Country: worldwide
Date: from pre-history
Size: 3 m (10 ft) long
Construction: wood
Speed: about 6 to 11 km/h (3½ to 7 mph)
On board: 2

Coracle

Shaped so that it can be carried on the back, the coracle is an early lightweight boat. The design drawback is that it is not very stable in the water. The user needs to be experienced to keep it under control having only a simple wooden spade-like paddle. Like the kayak and similar portable boats, it is still used, mainly for fishing.

Inuit kayak

Country: Canada
Date: from pre-history
Size: 5.5 m (18 ft) long
Construction: seal skin on wood or bone frame
Speed: about 6 to 11 km/h (3½ to 7 mph)
On board: 1

Wooden raft

The most basic water craft of all is the wooden raft. It is pushed along with a pole, and is made of several logs lashed together with creepers, twine or some other binding material. Early raft-builders realised quite quickly that their craft worked better if the logs had pointed ends, or if the entire raft front had a pointed shape.

Inuit kayak

For thousands of years the Inuit (Eskimo people of North America and Greenland) have built kayaks – long, narrow boats made of a wood or whalebone framework covered with skins. Kayaks are used for hunting and fishing, and their light weight makes them easy to carry. Their design makes them easy to return quickly to their upright position if they capsize.

Country: worldwide
Date: from pre-history
Size: 2 m (6½ ft) long
Construction: wood
Speed: about 6 to 11 km/h (3½ to 7 mph)
On board: 1 or more

Wooden raft

Pacific outrigger

This type of boat was built by the sailors of the Pacific islands. The outriggers gave the craft great stability on the Pacific surf, in spite of the narrow hull. This type of hull with its large sail could travel very fast, and early navigators covered thousands of kilometres in boats like these.

Pacific outrigger

Country: Polynesia, Micronesia
Date: from pre-history
Size: 9 m (30 ft) long
Construction: tree bark, strips of wood
Sail: cotton or matting
On board: 1 or more

Chinese junk

Country: China
Date: 9th century
Size: 6 to 137 m (20 to 250 ft)
Construction: wood
Sail: hemp or matting with bamboo battens
On board: 1 to 250

Chinese junk

The junk is the traditional Chinese sailing ship that evolved in medieval times. The hull is made differently from that of a Western ship. Instead of getting its strength from a keel, the hull is divided by bulkheads (wooden partitions) which make the structure rigid. The sails are made of narrow strips of cloth held on bamboo battens.

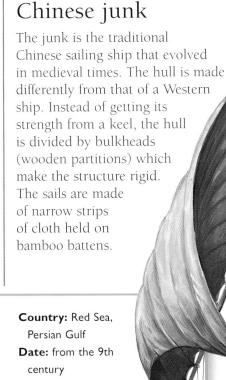

Country: Red Sea, Persian Gulf
Date: from the 9th century
Size: 40 m (131 ft)
Construction: wood
Sail: cotton or flax
On board: 18

Arab dhow

With their sleek wooden hulls, flat sterns and lateen (triangular) sails, the dhows of the Arab world are easy to recognise. They have one or two masts, and the lateen rig is especially good for sailing with winds from the side. They are used in the Red Sea, Indian Ocean and Persian Gulf. Some dhows now have diesel engines.

Arab dhow

Oars and sails

All early civilisations depended on sea and river transport. The ancient Egyptians travelled up and down the River Nile. The Greeks and Romans sailed all around the Mediterranean, relying on ships for both trade and war. These civilisations built the first sailing ships and developed the use of rows of oarsmen, who could propel a ship steadily and at speed over short distances. In addition, the Romans improved the steering oar, making their ships easier to move in battle.

Egyptian wooden boat

Egyptian wooden boat

Among the world's first sailing vessels was this Egyptian wooden-hulled, single-masted and square-sail boat. The rich used them to travel along the Nile. A steersman controlled the boat with a large oar at the rear, and there were also long poles which the crew could use to push the vessel off sand banks. Larger versions were used to carry cattle and other cargo.

Country: Egypt
Date: c.2000 BC
Size: 12 m (39 ft) long
Construction: cedar wood
Sail material: flax (linen)
On board: 10

Country: Greece
Date: c.480 BC
Size: 45 m (148 ft) long
Construction: wood
Sail material: flax (linen)
On board: 190

Greek trireme

Greek trireme

Sleek, fast and deadly, the Greek trireme was one of the most powerful warships of the ancient world. The term "trireme" means "three oars", and this type of ship had three tiers of oars – upper, middle and lower – on each side of the hull. Each oar was over 4 m (14 ft) long. Together with a square sail, this gave the trireme an impressive turn of speed – either to get out of trouble or to hole an enemy vessel with its fearsome ram.

Egyptian reed boat

Bundles of reeds were tied together with twine to make this early fishing boat. The papyrus reed – also used to make a paperlike writing material – was ideal for the job. It was light, easy to work, and grew plentifully by the banks of the Nile.

Egyptian reed boat

Country: Egypt
Date: c.3000 BC
Size: 20 m (6½ ft) long
Construction: papyrus reeds
Sail material: flax (linen)
On board: 4 or 5

Phoenician trader

The sea-trading Phoenicians built broad and deep-framed ships to carry cargoes of cloth and glassware around the Mediterranean. Their ships could have sails, oars or both. Their timber construction was very sturdy and these vessels voyaged as far as Cornwall and Ireland.

Phoenician trader

Country: Mediterranean area
Date: c.1200 BC
Size: from 25 m (82 ft) long
Construction: wood
Sail material: flax (linen)
On board: 30

Roman galley

Roman warships were called galleys, and they could have two or three tiers of oars. The oarsmen were usually slaves or criminals. The Roman navy also used sails for extra speed, and they attacked their enemies by ramming. Galleys would also come alongside and throw out a wooden bridge for soldiers to swarm on to enemy ships.

Roman galley

Country: Mediterranean area
Date: 1st century BC
Size: 45 m (148 ft) long
Construction: wood
Sail material: flax (linen)
On board: 120

Roman merchantman

Roman merchantman

The Romans needed large ships to carry goods around their huge empire. Their merchant ships were solidly built and broad. With one mast, usually rigged with a single, square sail, they were not very fast. However, they could carry up to 250 tonnes of cargo. There was extra space and height on the "poop deck" (aft).

Country: Mediterranean area
Date: 1st century BC
Size: 30 m (98 ft) long
Construction: wood
Sail material: flax (linen)
On board: 30

Viking longship

These elegant ships with their decorated prows were feared for bringing Vikings on raids along the coasts of Europe. All had a single mast, a square sail, and up to 34 ports for oars on each side. Smaller versions were used along rivers and broader ones for cargo.

Viking longship

Country: Northern Europe area
Date: c.850 AD
Size: from 21 m (69 ft) long
Construction: wood
Sail material: wool
On board: 34

Sailing to new worlds

Sailing the uncharted oceans in the 1400s was like travelling to the planets today. Carracks, caravels and similar sailing ships took European navigators to new worlds. Early sailing ships were small with square sails and lateen (triangular) sails, and sometimes both. The three-masted, square-rigged ship remained little changed for several hundred years.

Caravel

Cog

Country: Northern Europe
Date: 13th to 15th centuries
Size: 25 m (82 ft) long
Construction: wood
Sail material: flax or hemp
On board: 12

Cog

A sturdy cargo vessel, the cog was steered with a rudder, which hung from a straight stern post. There were small raised decks, called the forecastle and after castle, at either end of the ship. The sail was square.

Caravel

This type of ship was favoured by many of the great Portuguese and Spanish explorers, including Christopher Columbus. The caravel was quite narrow and light in weight. It had a square stern and a curved prow. A caravel usually had three masts and these were rigged with triangular sails, which could take advantage of side winds. Some caravels also carried a square sail.

Country: Portugal, Spain
Date: 15th and 16th centuries
Size: 40 m (131 ft) long
Construction: wood
Sail material: flax or hemp
On board: 40

Carrack

Country: Southern Europe
Date: 15th and 16th centuries
Size: 30 m (98 ft) long
Construction: wood
Sail material: flax or hemp
On board: 25 to 40

Carrack

These could be ships of over 1,000 tonnes, carrying a large load of cargo because their hulls were deep and high-sided. They were also very strong, with as many as four long reinforcing timbers, called wales, running along the length of the hull. Carracks usually had three masts (sometimes four), the main mast being much taller than the others. They were also used as warships.

Galleon

Galleons were tall fighting ships with elegant, pointed prows and high after castles that could be decorated with rich carving and gilding. They carried rows of cannons, which fired through square gun ports on the sides of the ship. The extra weight of these heavy guns could have made the galleon unstable, but the ship's inward-sloping sides helped keep it steady.

Country: Europe
Date: 17th century
Size: 38 m (125 ft) long
Construction: wood
Sail material: flax or hemp
On board: 142

Galleon

Country: Southern Europe
Date: 15th and 16th centuries
Size: 40 m (131 ft) long
Construction: wood, clinker built
Sail material: flax or hemp
On board: 40 or more

Mayflower

The *Mayflower* was similar to a small galleon, but with only a handful of guns. The decks were used for cramming in supplies and passengers who were the early settlers of North America, known as the Pilgrims. The crew had a cabin and galley in the forecastle.

Mayflower

Pinnace

Smaller than a galleon, a pinnace could be either rowed or sailed. It was a three-masted vessel with a large after castle and a tapering prow. The ship was square-rigged, but the rear mast could be rigged with just a triangular sail.

Pinnace

Dutch East Indiaman

Country: Northern Europe
Date: 13th to 15th centuries
Size: 25 m (82 ft) long
Construction: wood
Sail material: flax or hemp
On board: 12

Dutch East Indiaman

The islands of Indonesia were known as the Spice Islands or the East Indies. Many European merchants traded there and in China and India. They used *East Indiamen* to bring back their cargoes. The ships had large hulls with plenty of cargo space. They had three masts and also carried many guns on their upper decks to protect themselves against attack.

Country: Northern Europe
Date: 17th and 18th centuries
Size: 45 m (148 ft) long
Construction: wood
Sail material: flax or hemp
On board: 45 or more

Big sailing ships

From the 17th century, seafaring nations such as Britain and Holland began to acquire large worldwide empires. They needed larger ships to carry all sorts of cargoes – spices, tea, slaves and sugar – to and from their colonies across the oceans. These bigger ships also carried more sails, making them faster and more manoeuvrable. Some of these vessels, such as the clippers, could sail from London to Shanghai in under 100 days.

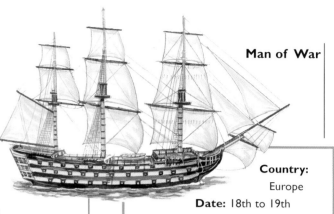

Man of War

Country: Europe
Date: 18th to 19th centuries
Size: 120 m (394 ft) long
Construction: wood
Sail fabric: flax or hemp
On board: 800

Man of War

These warships usually had one to three decks of cannons. A three-decker could carry over 100 guns. They were designed to get the captain within range of the enemy so that a "broadside" of cannonballs could be fired.

Endeavour

Endeavour

British Captain James Cook set off in 1768 for his explorations to the Pacific in a ship originally designed to carry coal in the rough North Sea. The solidly-built *Endeavour* had plenty of room in the hold for supplies, plant specimens, carvings and other items Cook collected.

Country: Europe
Date: 18th century
Size: 40 m (131 ft) long
Construction: wood
Sail fabric: flax or hemp
On board: 90

Frigate

Country: USA
Date: 19th century
Size: 55 m (180 ft) long
Construction: wood
Sail fabric: cotton or hemp
On board: 28

Frigate

Frigates carry their main weapons on a single deck. The US Navy designed large and speedy frigates to defend shipping from attacks by pirates – especially Barbary corsairs from North Africa. Some American frigates had 44 guns.

Thomas W Lawson

A schooner is a sailing ship with two or more masts and the lower sails rigged along the length of the vessel. Most were coastal or medium-range cargo vessels but some were huge ocean-going schooners. The *Thomas W Lawson* is the biggest ever built. She had seven masts but used engines to help a very small crew hoist her sails.

Thomas W Lawson

Country: USA
Date: 1902
Size: 120 m (395 ft) long
Construction: wood planking on iron
Sail fabric: flax or hemp
On board: about 20

Barquentine

Square sails on the foremast and fore-and-aft rigging on the two rear masts identify barquentines. Rather long in proportion to their depth, they were graceful vessels. Because they had fewer square sails they required smaller crews than full-rigged ships. They were popular in the Pacific when they were introduced in the 1830s, and were frequently seen on the Great Lakes of North America and canals that connected them.

Country: Europe, USA
Date: late 19th century
Size: 100 m (328 ft) long
Construction: wood or steel
Sail fabric: flax, cotton or hemp
On board: 30

Barquentine

Country: Europe, USA
Date: late 19th century
Size: 100 m (328 ft) long
Construction: steel
Sail fabric: flax, cotton or hemp
On board: 30

Four-masted barque

Ships like this continued to sail in the age of steam. They were large, square-sterned and carried plenty of sail. Seamen gave the name "barque" to any vessel with non-square sails, rigged fore-and-aft (lengthways) on the mizzen (rearmost) mast.

Clipper

The clippers were the transport record-breakers of their day. They were built to carry cargo at speed – supplies to the new communities of the California gold rush and tea from China to Europe. Clippers had sleek bows, long narrow hulls and up to about 2,790 sq m (30,000 sq ft) of sail. They could cover long distances in shorter times than any other sailing ship, for example from Melbourne to London in under 80 days.

Four-masted barque

Clipper

Country: USA, Europe
Date: late 18th and 19th centuries
Size: 110 m (361 ft) long
Construction: wood and iron
Sail fabric: flax, hemp or cotton
On board: 45

Full steam ahead

For thousands of years, ships could only steer a course that the wind or oar power allowed. Then in the 19th century, the steam engine brought about a mechanical revolution in sea transport. Steamships could steer almost any course at any time, and at a regular speed. The first steamship, *Pyroscaphe*, was built in France in 1783. Early steamships had paddle wheels. Propellers took over in the 1840s. Sails continued to be carried until the 1860s, when marine engines had become more reliable.

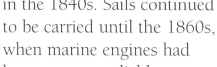

Charlotte Dundas

Country: UK
Date: 1801
Size: 17.7 m (58 ft) long
Construction: wood
Top speed: 6.5 km/h (4 mph)
On board: 6

Charlotte Dundas

The first practical steamship, the *Charlotte Dundas*, towed barges on the River Clyde in Scotland for three or four weeks in 1802. It was powered by a single-cylinder 12 horsepower engine driving a paddle wheel. The vessel was taken out of service because of damage to the river banks caused by the wash from its paddle wheel.

Great Western

The *Great Western* was built of oak and designed by Isambard Kingdom Brunel in 1837. It had four steam engines driving both paddle wheels and a propeller and was the first ship to have enough coal for a non-stop voyage. It set out on its first transatlantic voyage on 8 April 1838 and docked in New York 15 days and 5 hours later.

Country: UK
Date: 1837
Size: 72 m (236 ft) long
Construction: wood, iron reinforcements
Top speed: 15.75 km/h (10 mph)
On board: 148

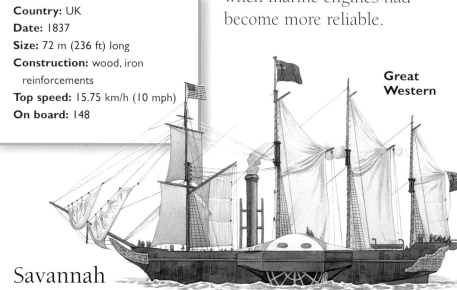

Great Western

Savannah

The *Savannah* was the first steamship to cross the Atlantic Ocean. It was a sailing vessel fitted with steam engines and paddle wheels. It made its historic voyage from Savannah, Georgia, USA to Liverpool in 27 days. Its wood-burning engines were used to drive two paddle wheels for only a small part of the crossing but enough to prove that steamships were practical ocean-going vessels.

Savannah

Country: USA
Date: 1819
Size: 30 m (98½ ft) long
Construction: wood
Top speed: 15 km/h (9 mph)
On board: 42

Country: UK
Date: 1838
Size: 211 m (692 ft) long
Construction: wood
Top speed: 24 km/h (15 mph)
On board: 3,500

Britannia

Britannia

Britannia was a wooden paddle steamer and the first transatlantic passenger liner. Its ocean service began in 1840. As part of a fleet of passenger steamers, it offered a twice-monthly passage all year round between Liverpool and Boston.

Country: UK
Date: 1840
Size: 64.7 m (212 ft) long
Construction: wood
Top speed: 15.75 km/h (10 mph)
On board: 204

Country: UK
Date: 1856
Size: 115 m (377 ft) long
Construction: iron
Top speed: 25 km/h (15½ mph)
On board: 250

Persia

Great Britain

Brunel's second transatlantic ship was also the first iron-hulled steamship. He designed it with paddle wheels but these were changed for a propeller. In 1970, its rusting hull was brought to Bristol docks, where it was originally built, and restored.

Persia

The *Persia* was the world's largest liner until the *Great Eastern* was built. It was also one of the last to be powered by paddles – they were huge at 12 m (40 ft) across – rather than by a screw propeller.

Great Eastern

When the *Great Eastern* was built it was five times the size of any other ship. It was powered by a screw propeller and paddle wheels, and carried enough coal to reach Australia without refuelling. It failed as a liner but successfully laid the first transatlantic telegraph cable in 1866 on its second attempt.

Country: UK
Date: 1843
Size: 98 m (322 ft) long
Construction: iron
Top speed: 20 km/h (13 mph)
On board: 260

Great Britain

Great Eastern

Luxury liners

Steamships began carrying passengers and mail across the Atlantic from 1838. By the 1890s liners were designed to accommodate hundreds of passengers in the sort of luxury usually found in the best hotels. Swimming pools, dance-floors, opulent lounges and restaurants catered to the wealthy first-class travellers. Below water, a row of watertight bulkheads (walls) stretched across each vessel, dividing it into separate compartments to keep it afloat if one part of the hull was damaged. Modern cruise ships carry 4.5 million people every year.

Turbinia

This was the first vessel to be driven by a steam turbine. In this type of engine, high-pressure steam pushes on a series of blades that are fixed to a metal shaft. When the blades move, the shaft turns, making the ship's propeller spin around.

Turbinia

Country: UK
Date: 1894
Size: 32 m (105 ft) long
Construction: steel
Top speed: 61 km/h (32¾ mph)
On board: 5

Country: UK
Date: 1901
Size: 100 m (328 ft) long
Construction: steel
Top speed: 38 km/h (23½ mph)
On board: 200

King Edward

The first merchant ship to be powered by the kind of turbines used in the *Turbinia* was the *King Edward*. The vessel's powerful engines propelled the ship on passenger services up and down the River Clyde and on cruises along the Scottish coast. The ship was used to carry troops during World War II before being broken up in 1952.

King Edward

Titanic

With interiors based on a French royal palace, the *Titanic* was very luxurious. It was the largest ship of the time. But on 12 April 1912, its maiden voyage, it hit an iceberg and sank in the Atlantic Ocean, off the coast of New Foundland. There were too few lifeboats and 1,500 people drowned. Now all ships have to carry enough lifeboats and life jackets for all those on board.

Titanic

Bremen

The German-built *Bremen* was designed to be the fastest transatlantic liner. The record had been set 20 years before by Britain's *Mauretania* at 48 km/h (26 mph). *Bremen* beat the record. It was also more spacious than its rival, with an extra 40 m (131 ft) of hull space for the same number of passengers and crew.

Country: Germany
Date: 1929
Size: 286 m (938 ft) long
Construction: steel
Top speed: 52 km/h (28 mph)
On board: 2,990

Bremen

Country: UK
Date: 1912
Size: 260 m (853 ft) long
Construction: steel
Top speed: 41 km/h (22 mph)
On board: 3,511

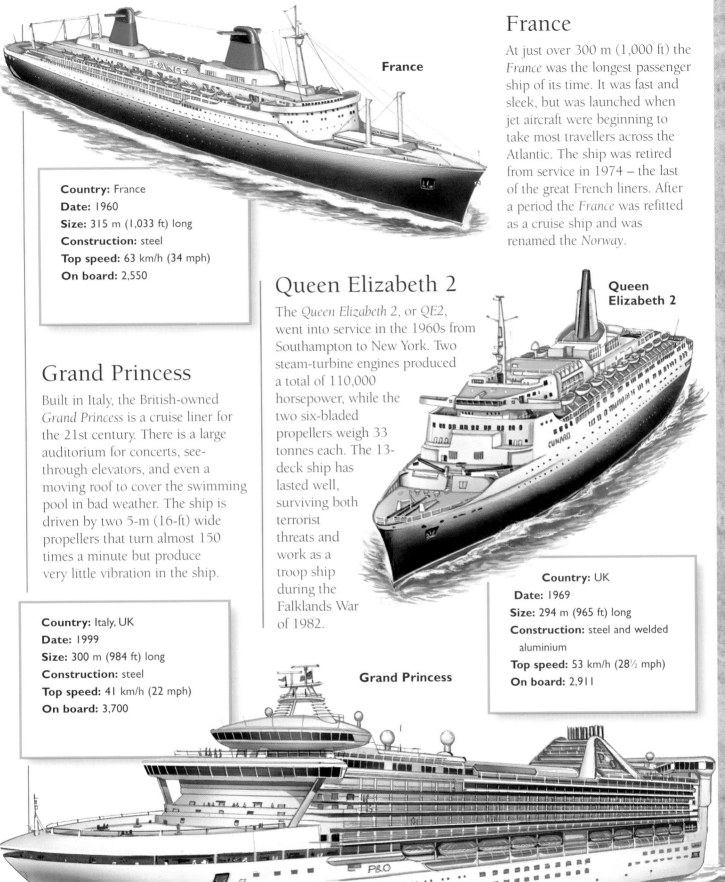

France

At just over 300 m (1,000 ft) the *France* was the longest passenger ship of its time. It was fast and sleek, but was launched when jet aircraft were beginning to take most travellers across the Atlantic. The ship was retired from service in 1974 – the last of the great French liners. After a period the *France* was refitted as a cruise ship and was renamed the *Norway*.

France

Country: France
Date: 1960
Size: 315 m (1,033 ft) long
Construction: steel
Top speed: 63 km/h (34 mph)
On board: 2,550

Grand Princess

Built in Italy, the British-owned *Grand Princess* is a cruise liner for the 21st century. There is a large auditorium for concerts, see-through elevators, and even a moving roof to cover the swimming pool in bad weather. The ship is driven by two 5-m (16-ft) wide propellers that turn almost 150 times a minute but produce very little vibration in the ship.

Country: Italy, UK
Date: 1999
Size: 300 m (984 ft) long
Construction: steel
Top speed: 41 km/h (22 mph)
On board: 3,700

Queen Elizabeth 2

The *Queen Elizabeth 2*, or QE2, went into service in the 1960s from Southampton to New York. Two steam-turbine engines produced a total of 110,000 horsepower, while the two six-bladed propellers weigh 33 tonnes each. The 13-deck ship has lasted well, surviving both terrorist threats and work as a troop ship during the Falklands War of 1982.

Queen Elizabeth 2

Country: UK
Date: 1969
Size: 294 m (965 ft) long
Construction: steel and welded aluminium
Top speed: 53 km/h (28½ mph)
On board: 2,911

Grand Princess

Fighting ships

With the coming of steam power, the way the warships looked and operated changed. Sails and wooden hulls were replaced with screw propellers and iron hulls. Warships became faster, easier to manoeuvre, and had more space for newer and bigger guns that fired explosive shells. Modern navies use a variety of different craft, from huge aircraft carriers to nuclear-powered submarines and smaller multi-task ships.

Warrior

Driven by both steam and sail, the *Warrior* was the first ocean-going iron-clad battleship in the world. Thick armoured plates were bolted to a teak hull to give massive protection. The ship also carried 36 powerful guns making it the most heavily armed ship at the time.

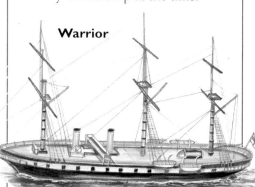
Warrior

Country: UK
Date: 1859
Size: 116 m (420 ft) long
Construction: wood, iron armour
Top speed: 31.5 km/h (17 mph)
On board: 707

Merrimack

Monitor

Merrimack vs Monitor

The US Civil War between the Northern and Southern states (1861–65) saw the first battle between metal-armoured, steam-driven ships. The North's all-iron battleship *Monitor* lay low in the water, bearing a single turret with two guns. The South's *Merrimack* was fitted with sloping iron armour over its deck.

Country: USA
Date: 1862
Size: *Monitor* 52 m (172 ft) long;
  Merrimack 80 m (263 ft) long
Construction: wood, iron armour
Top speed: *Monitor* 11 km/h (6 mph);
  Merrimack 17 km/h (9 mph)
On board: *Monitor* 49;
  Merrimack 330

Dreadnought

The steel-plated *Dreadnought* was the first modern battleship. It had heavy guns mounted on five turrets that could be fired at the same time. A telephone linked each turret to a control platform.

Lightning

Torpedo missiles which travel underwater to their target were developed in the 1860s and 1870s. Navies quickly set about building ships to fire torpedoes. The *Lightning* was one of the first British torpedo boats and was also used to defend coastal bases from enemy attack.

Lightning

Country: UK
Date: 1877
Size: 26 m (84 ft) long
Construction: wood
Top speed: 33 km/h (20 mph)
On board: 35

Country: UK
Date: 1906
Size: 160 m (526 ft) long
Construction: steel
Top speed: 39 km/h (21 mph)
On board: 773

Dreadnought

Yamato

In the late 1930s this vast Japanese World War II battleship was the largest-ever warship – only the liner *Queen Mary* was heavier. The ship could therefore have many guns. On the main turrets alone there were nine guns, each of which could fire two heavy shells per minute up to a distance of 40 km (25 miles).

Yamato

Country: Japan
Date: 1937
Size: 263 m (862 ft) long
Construction: steel
Top speed: 50 km/h (27 mph)
On board: 2,500

MEKO-class frigate

Escort vessels, such as the MEKO series, are used to protect aircraft carriers, groups of submarines or convoys of ships. The name is an abbreviation for a German word meaning "multi-purpose". The basic hull is designed so that different weapons and equipment can be fitted when needed.

Country: Germany
Date: 1980s
Size: 91.2 m (299 ft) long
Construction: steel
Top speed: 50 km/h (27 mph)
On board: 90

MEKO-class frigate

USS Virginia

The warship USS *Virginia* was powered by a nuclear reactor. The reactor heats water to produce steam, which drives a turbine as in a regular steamship. The advantage of nuclear power is that the vessel can sail vast distances without having to stop for fuel: one fuelling alone can take such a ship three times around the world. However, there is a big safety risk, in spite of the fact that on-board reactors have protective shields weighing as much as 1,000 tonnes. In addition, only a few specialised depots can make repairs to this type of ship.

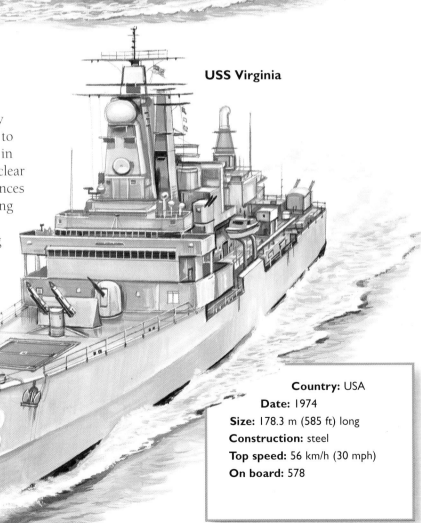

USS Virginia

Country: USA
Date: 1974
Size: 178.3 m (585 ft) long
Construction: steel
Top speed: 56 km/h (30 mph)
On board: 578

Powerboats

Water-jet engine

A water-jet engine takes in water through a duct and forces it out at speed and at high pressure, through the stern of the unit. The result is that the boat is pushed forwards in the opposite direction to the jet of water.

Round-the-world powered record

The slender hull of the *Cable & Wireless Adventurer* is designed to slice through the waves at up to 28 km/h (45 mph). Its twin turbo-diesel engines are powerful and efficient, cutting down the need for refuelling. With 16 crew members, the 35-m (115-ft), 52-tonne powerboat set off in April 1998 to break the round-the-world record for a motor-powered vessel. It took 75 days and the craft had cut 9 days off the previous record.

Powered craft can be anything from a small dinghy with an outboard motor to a high-speed racing vessel. But for most people a "powerboat" means a racing craft built for speeds of up to 90 km/h (57 mph) or more. There are many types, but most are made with planing hulls – in other words, they are designed to rise up out of the water as they pick up speed, to reduce drag and help them go even faster. They are often built with modern materials, such as layers of fibreglass sandwiched with lightweight balsa wood. This cuts down weight and improves performance still further.

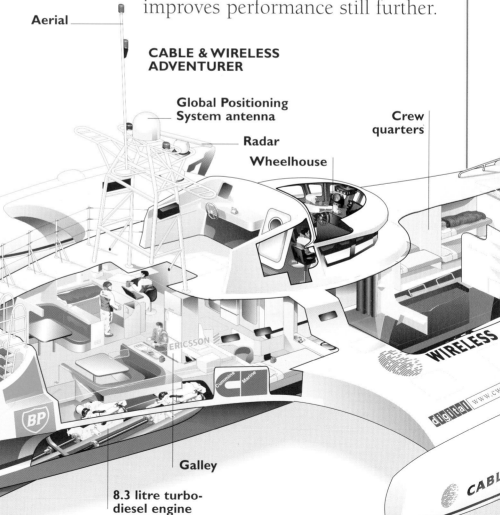

Aerial

CABLE & WIRELESS ADVENTURER

Global Positioning System antenna

Radar

Wheelhouse

Crew quarters

Rubber dinghy

Galley

8.3 litre turbo-diesel engine

Propeller

Rudders

62

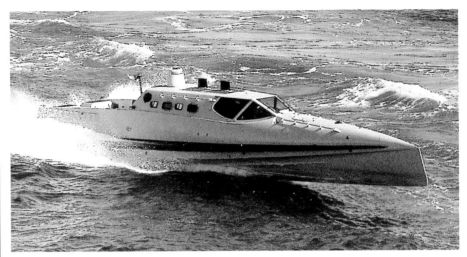

VSVs

The *VSV* (Very Slender Vessel) is a powerboat with a long, thin hull with deep and narrow sides. These give both stability and sharp turning in the water. The *VSV* tends to push or pierce its way in and under the waves rather than riding over them, which makes its passage both fast and smooth. The vessel is designed to be used by coastal police patrols and special military forces.

Hull shapes

Powerboat hulls are designed to offer little resistance as they move through the water, so that they can reach the highest possible speeds. One way to achieve this is to make a very slim single hull, or monohull, that slices through the waves. Creating a twin-hulled boat, or catamaran, also cuts down the amount of contact between hulls and water, reducing friction. Hydroplanes solve the problem by rising right up out of the water, skimming over the surface with the least drag, or resistance.

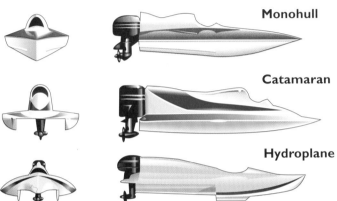

Monohull

Catamaran

Hydroplane

Powerboat types

Powerboats can be pleasure craft designed to carry one or more people and to give them a taste of speed. Offshore racers go faster, and even monohull designs lift out of the water as they reach top speed. Hydroplanes race at speeds of over 160 km/h (100 mph) while the powerful Formula One craft have 300 horsepower engines capable of 200 km/h (125 mph) and sharp right-angled turns.

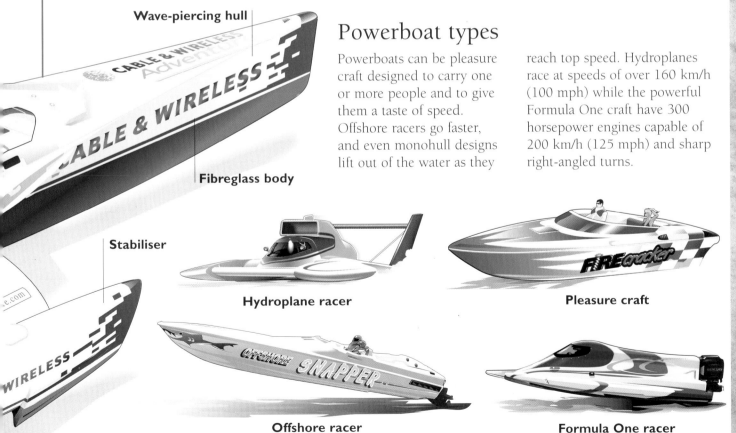

Wave-piercing hull

Fibreglass body

Stabiliser

Hydroplane racer

Pleasure craft

Offshore racer

Formula One racer

Underwater vessels

Any submarine craft needs a strong hull to withstand the pressure deep underwater, and a tube-shaped design to cut through it with least resistance. The largest underwater craft are nuclear submarines with powerful engines that can travel far away from base without refuelling. Smaller underwater vessels, known as submersibles, are used for scientific and shipwreck exploration, as well as for checking oil rigs and making repairs below the water.

Nautilus

Country: USA
Date: 1800
Size: 6.4 m (21 ft) long
Construction: iron framework, copper outer covering
Top speed: 6.5 km/h (4 mph) underwater
On board: 3

Nautilus

This strange craft, was powered by sail on the surface and by a hand-cranked propeller underwater. It was invented by American Robert Fulton, and tested in France, where it stayed underwater for an hour. The aim was to use *Nautilus* to attach explosives to the hulls of enemy ships, but the craft was never used in naval warfare.

Holland No. 6

Country: USA
Date: 1897
Size: 16.3 m (153 ft) long
Construction: iron
Top speed: 15 km/h (9 mph) underwater
On board: 7

Holland No. 6

Irish-American engineer James Holland's *No. 6* was called a "monster war fish" in the American press. It was the first modern submarine, and boasted ballast tanks, torpedo tubes, and a periscope that could be retracted when the craft dived (features that were used on nearly all the later submarines). It had hydroplanes (fins) to help move up and down.

Country: France
Date: 1893
Size: 48.5 m (159 ft) long
Construction: copper
Top speed: 12 km/h (7½ mph) underwater
On board: 19

Gustave Zédé

This was the first submarine to be fitted with a periscope, which allowed the captain and the crew to view the surface of the water while they were still submerged. One of the first effective submarines, this sleek vessel was driven by an electric motor powered by huge batteries.

Gustave Zédé

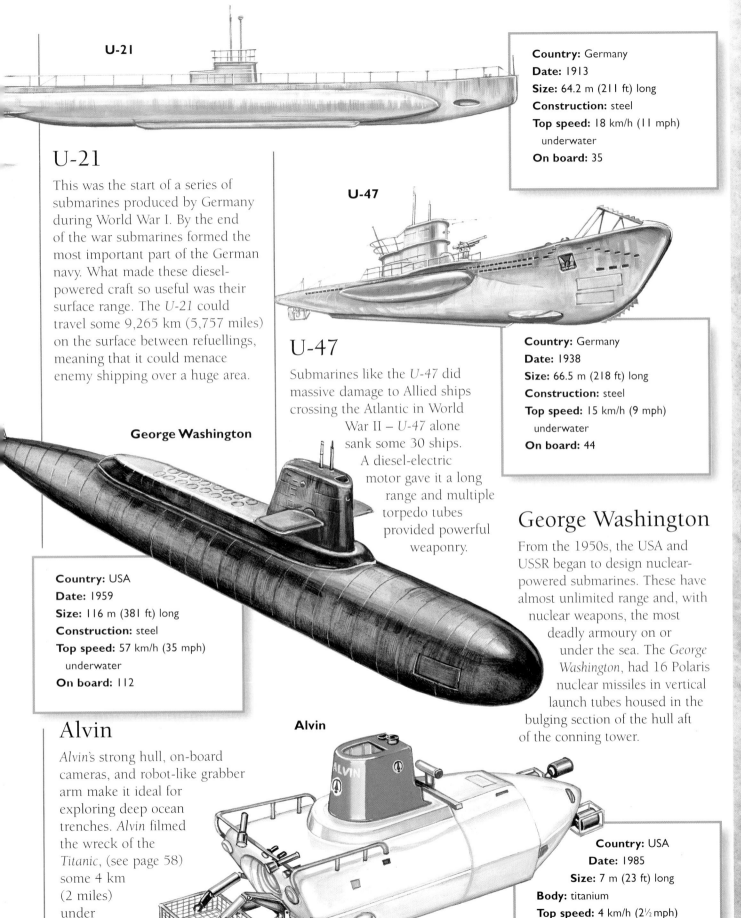

U-21

U-21

This was the start of a series of submarines produced by Germany during World War I. By the end of the war submarines formed the most important part of the German navy. What made these diesel-powered craft so useful was their surface range. The *U-21* could travel some 9,265 km (5,757 miles) on the surface between refuellings, meaning that it could menace enemy shipping over a huge area.

Country: Germany
Date: 1913
Size: 64.2 m (211 ft) long
Construction: steel
Top speed: 18 km/h (11 mph) underwater
On board: 35

U-47

U-47

Submarines like the *U-47* did massive damage to Allied ships crossing the Atlantic in World War II – *U-47* alone sank some 30 ships. A diesel-electric motor gave it a long range and multiple torpedo tubes provided powerful weaponry.

Country: Germany
Date: 1938
Size: 66.5 m (218 ft) long
Construction: steel
Top speed: 15 km/h (9 mph) underwater
On board: 44

George Washington

George Washington

From the 1950s, the USA and USSR began to design nuclear-powered submarines. These have almost unlimited range and, with nuclear weapons, the most deadly armoury on or under the sea. The *George Washington*, had 16 Polaris nuclear missiles in vertical launch tubes housed in the bulging section of the hull aft of the conning tower.

Country: USA
Date: 1959
Size: 116 m (381 ft) long
Construction: steel
Top speed: 57 km/h (35 mph) underwater
On board: 112

Alvin

Alvin's strong hull, on-board cameras, and robot-like grabber arm make it ideal for exploring deep ocean trenches. *Alvin* filmed the wreck of the *Titanic*, (see page 58) some 4 km (2 miles) under the sea.

Alvin

Country: USA
Date: 1985
Size: 7 m (23 ft) long
Body: titanium
Top speed: 4 km/h (2½ mph) underwater
On board: 3

Cargo carriers

Ships that carry cargo are called merchant ships, and there are a huge variety of these vessels on the seas today. They range from vast oil tankers to tiny tugs, from car-carrying ferries to ships specially built to recover other damaged ships. They may be slow but they can carry much larger amounts of goods and raw materials than any other form of transport – and at very low costs – anywhere in the world. Cargo ships have very little super-structure (the part above the main deck level). There is a navigation bridge with funnels, and the engines and crew accommodation below. The rest of the ship holds as much cargo as possible.

Gas tanker

When gases are refrigerated under pressure they turn to liquid. Large gas tankers, carrying liquid gas in big, spherical tanks, became common during the 1970s. Such tankers can contain up to 125,000 cubic metres of liquid gas. These ships ply the oceans, notably between Australia and Japan.

Gas tanker

Country: Netherlands
Date: 1973
Size: 97 m (318 ft) long
Construction: steel
Top speed: 22 km/h (12 mph)
On board: 20

Country:
  Norway
Date: 1978
Size: 450 m (1,475 ft) long
Construction: steel
Top speed: 26 km/h (14 mph)
On board: 18

Supertanker

Supertanker

The world's largest ships can weigh half a million tonnes and are so huge that they need several kilometres to slow down and stop. They carry oil in several vast tanks which have to be separated to prevent the oil surging in heavy seas and possible capsizing.

Container ship

Instead of carrying all sorts of goods of many awkward shapes, container vessels carry 6-m or 12-m (20-ft or 40-ft) long metal containers, which fit exactly on to both ships and lorries. The strong containers are stacked in piles of up to 13 and each container can take as much as 21.7 tonnes of cargo.

Container ship

Country: Spain
Date: 1974
Size: 91 m (300 ft) long
Construction: steel
Top speed: 26 km/h (14 mph)
On board: 20

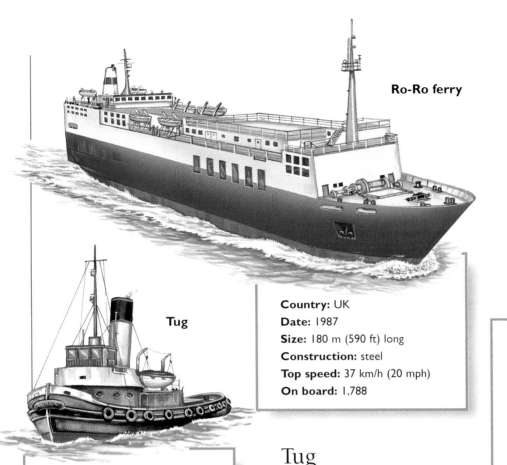

Ro-Ro ferry

Ships that accommodated motor vehicles, allowing you to drive on and off are called "roll-on roll-off" or ro-ro vessels. They are used widely all over the world to carry all sorts of traffic from lorries loaded with cargo to cars and their passengers. A typical larger ro-ro ship has a series of car decks with access at either end. Above are decks that offer lounges, restaurants and other passenger facilities.

Country: UK
Date: 1987
Size: 180 m (590 ft) long
Construction: steel
Top speed: 37 km/h (20 mph)
On board: 1,788

Country: France
Date: 1994
Size: 32 m (105 ft) long
Construction: steel
Top speed: 20 km/h (11 mph)
On board: 7

Country: Netherlands
Date: 1973
Size: 97 m (318 ft) long
Construction: steel
Top speed: 22 km/h (12 mph)
On board: 20

Tug

With the rise of the steam engine, tugs were built to tow sailing ships in and out of port, when the wind was not favourable. Soon tugs were being used for other tasks, such as towing barges, helping large ships to dock, for fire-fighting and helping broken down boats.

Pontoon barge

How do you transport a damaged ship across the sea? By using a heavy-lift ship called a pontoon barge. It has a long, low deck with tanks that can be filled with water or pumped out. As the barge sinks below sea level the damaged vessel is floated on board.

Salvage vessel

Ships that have accidents at sea are often brought in by salvage vessels. Such ships are longer and more suited to sailing on the open sea than tugs (which stay close to coasts and ports). For better steering, they may have nozzle mounted propellers that can be aimed in any direction.

Country: Germany
Date: 1990
Size: 156 m (512 ft) long
Construction: steel
Top speed: 27 km/h (14½ mph)
On board: 23

Surface skimmers

For many years, boat builders have realised that if you lift a craft's hull out of the water, you reduce drag, allowing the vessel to travel more quickly. The first vessels to use this idea were hydrofoils, which raise the hull on stilts called foils. A hovercraft works differently, blowing a cushion of air under the hull, so that the craft is just above the water surface. Another design is the catamaran, which has slim twin hulls that lie in the water, and a broad body raised above the surface between the hulls.

Hovercraft SR.N1

The hovercraft was invented by British engineer, Christopher Cockerell, in 1955. Four years later, the first full-size working version impressed onlookers with its speed and its ability to turn on its own axis, and even to reverse.

Hovercraft SR.N1

Country: UK
Date: 1959
Size: 12.5 m (41 ft) long
Construction: steel
Top speed: 111 km/h (70 mph)
On board: 1

Hovercraft SR.N4

Hovercraft SR.N4

The original *SR.N4* appeared in 1968 and was the first hovercraft to offer a regular service across the English Channel. By the 1970s, a "stretched" version of the craft was in service, with more space for passengers and cars, and a deep skirt that could cushion the effects of waves at least 5 m (15 ft) high. Passengers like the *SR.N4* because it is fast – at least twice as quick as ordinary ferry boats.

Country: UK
Date: 1970 (Mark III model)
Size: 56 m (184 ft) long
Construction: steel, aluminium
Top speed: 111 km/h (70 mph)
On board: 400

Boeing Jetfoil

The foils of this craft lift it 2 m (6½ ft) in the air, allowing the *Jetfoil* to travel more than three times as fast as it can with its hull in the water like a normal boat. The vessel can also tilt like an aeroplane as it corners, making it more comfortable for those on board.

Country: USA
Date: 1975
Size: 27 m (89 ft) long
Construction: steel
Top speed: 83 km/h (52 mph)
On board: 240

Flying Dolphin

Flying Dolphin

This is one of the latest hydrofoils used for ferry work between the islands and mainland of Greece. Built in Australia like many vessels of this type, it combines speed, generous passenger space and comfort. The streamlined hull powers through the water, but when the foils lift it out, drag is reduced still further, allowing the boat to travel even more swiftly.

Country: Australia
Date: 1999
Size: 48 m (157 ft) long
Construction: steel
Top speed: 78 km/h (48 mph)
On board: 516

Boeing Jetfoil

Yamoto 1

Country: Japan
Date: 1992
Size: 30 m (98 ft) long
Construction: steel
Top speed: 15 km/h (9 mph)
On board: 3 crew

Yamoto 1

This experimental craft is propelled along by a tube in the water on the underside of the hull. The tube is surrounded by magnets to which an electric current is applied. This pushes the water through the tube at speed, forcing the boat along like a jet engine. The advantage is that the power unit has no moving parts to wear out or go wrong.

Country: Russia
Date: 1998
Size: 12 m (39 ft) long
Construction: aluminium
Top speed: 61 km/h (38 mph)
On board: 8

Czilim 20910

SeaCat

The *SeaCat* was the world's first catamaran designed to carry cars. Its twin-hull design is sleeker than ordinary car ferries, meaning that the vessel can skim through the water at speed. But the area between the dual hulls still gives the vessel plenty of breadth, so there is lots of space on board. The ship is powered by water jets and, in addition to the standard 74-m (243-ft) length, a larger *SeaCat* of 81-m (266-ft) is also in service.

Czilim 20910

Hovercraft are used by modern armed forces for their speed and agility. They can travel rapidly over shallow water or swampland, delivering troops to a trouble spot. This *Czilim* is a Russian border patrol vessel. The craft's twin diesel engines give it a range of about 480 km (300 miles).

Country: Australia
Date: 1990
Size: 74 m (243 ft) long
Construction: steel
Top speed: 69 km/h (43 mph)
On board: 598

SeaCat

Pleasure craft

People have enjoyed pleasure boating for hundreds of years, but its popularity has increased dramatically since World War II (1939–45). This has been made possible by the use of plywood, fibreglass and aluminium to make hulls which are tougher, lighter and cheaper than those made of wooden planking; also by improvements in sail-making and in outboard and inboard motors. More areas of water, such as man-made reservoirs, are also now available for sailing and for speedboats and jet skis.

Windsurfer

Basically a surfboard with a sail, windsurfers have been a popular sporting craft since they first appeared in 1969. Boarders can reach speeds of 80 km/h (50 mph) as they race or jump in competitions.

Windsurfer

Country: USA
Date: 1999 (this model)
Size: 2.7 m (9 ft) long
Construction: fibreglass
Sail material: artificial fibre
On board: 1

Optimist Dinghy

Country: USA
Date: 1980 (this model)
Size: 4 m (13 ft) long
Construction: polyurethane
  (high-strength plastic)
Sail material: artificial fibre
On board: 1

Sea Eagle

Inflatable dinghies are among the most versatile of all craft. Boats like this are used by sports divers, for fishing and in rescue work. Because they are so light and very buoyant they can travel very quickly when fitted with an outboard motor.

Optimist Dinghy

Many children have learnt to sail on this type of dinghy, originally designed in 1948. It is small and easy to transport, with a short single mast and a sliding daggerboard keel that allows the shallow hull to sail across the wind.

Jet ski

The "personal watercraft" or jet ski is like a water-borne motorbike and is just as powerful and noisy. A jet ski carries the driver close to the water. Designers are starting to create models that are not so loud, and make less of an impact on the shore environment.

Sea Eagle

Country: USA
Date: 1998
Size: 3.2 m (10½ ft) long
Construction: reinforced
  man-made fibre
Speed: 46 km/h (28½ mph)
On board: 5

Jet ski

Country: Japan
Date: 1999 (this model)
Size: 2.7 m (9 ft) long
Construction: reinforced
  fibreglass
Speed: 95 km/h (58 mph)
On board: 2

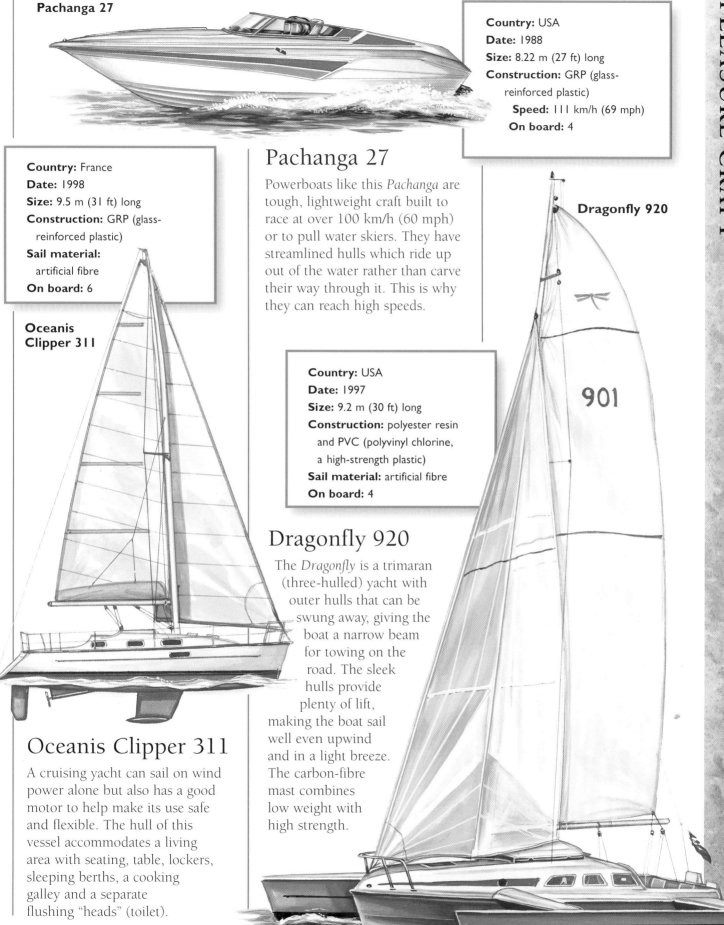

Pachanga 27

Country: USA
Date: 1988
Size: 8.22 m (27 ft) long
Construction: GRP (glass-reinforced plastic)
Speed: 111 km/h (69 mph)
On board: 4

Pachanga 27

Powerboats like this *Pachanga* are tough, lightweight craft built to race at over 100 km/h (60 mph) or to pull water skiers. They have streamlined hulls which ride up out of the water rather than carve their way through it. This is why they can reach high speeds.

Country: France
Date: 1998
Size: 9.5 m (31 ft) long
Construction: GRP (glass-reinforced plastic)
Sail material: artificial fibre
On board: 6

Oceanis Clipper 311

Dragonfly 920

Country: USA
Date: 1997
Size: 9.2 m (30 ft) long
Construction: polyester resin and PVC (polyvinyl chlorine, a high-strength plastic)
Sail material: artificial fibre
On board: 4

Dragonfly 920

The *Dragonfly* is a trimaran (three-hulled) yacht with outer hulls that can be swung away, giving the boat a narrow beam for towing on the road. The sleek hulls provide plenty of lift, making the boat sail well even upwind and in a light breeze. The carbon-fibre mast combines low weight with high strength.

Oceanis Clipper 311

A cruising yacht can sail on wind power alone but also has a good motor to help make its use safe and flexible. The hull of this vessel accommodates a living area with seating, table, lockers, sleeping berths, a cooking galley and a separate flushing "heads" (toilet).

New horizons

Ever since the first boats took to water, the challenge for the adventurous sailor has been to travel faster and further. The great age of racing began in the 19th century when wealthy enthusiasts started to build yachts especially for this. Racing yachts today use space-age materials for everything from keels to sails and rely on satellite navigation to find their way. Technological improvements mean people can attempt new feats such as solo round-the-world races, breaking speed records or using mostly muscle power to cross oceans.

Francis Chichester began yacht racing in 1953. By 1960 he had won the first ever solo yacht race across the Atlantic Ocean in his boat **Gipsy Moth III**. He followed up this triumph in 1966–67 with the first solo voyage around the world in **Gipsy Moth IV**, taking a total of 226 days.

Donald Campbell was one of the world's great speed-record breakers. In 1964, driving his hydroplane **Bluebird**, he reached 444.7 km/h (276¼ mph) on Lake Dumbleyung, Australia. He was killed in 1967 when his boat crashed at 515 km/h (320 mph).

Jason Lewis is the first person to pedal round the world. Part of his trip was overland but he also completed the first crossing of the Pacific in a pedal-powered boat in August 2000. **Moksha** is only 8 m (26 ft) long with a cabin the size of a small wardrobe. Solar panels power a computer, a satellite telephone and a Global Positioning System.

The most sought-after prize in yacht racing, the America's Cup is named after the yacht that first won it in 1851. This elegant J-class schooner, **Endeavour**, just failed to win the cup in 1934.

The SeaCat **Hoverspeed Great Britain** travelled across the Atlantic Ocean in 3 days 7 hours and 54 minutes in 1990 – the fastest-ever crossing.

The first boat in the gruelling Whitbread Round-the-World Race to have an all-woman crew was **Maiden**, a 17.5-m (57-ft) sloop. Many said the 51,500-km (31,980-mile) race was too hard for women but skipper **Tracy Edwards** and her crew proved them wrong. They not only finished the 1989 race but won two of the stages in their class.

On the tracks

Railways are the most efficient way to move large numbers of people and heavy cargoes, and they cause the least damage to the environment.

The first railways were simple grooved tracks, carved in stone blocks and used in Babylon in about 2245 BC. Later, horses dragged coal wagons along simple wooden rails until the invention of the steam locomotive 200 years ago. Today a modern freight train hauled by a diesel or electric locomotive can do the same job as over 50 lorries, and a high-speed passenger train can carry the same number of people as 200 cars, in greater comfort and at higher speeds.

Burlington Zephyr 1934

Powerful steel wheels with connecting and coupling rods help drive this **Chinese steam locomotive**. China has more railway lines than anywhere in the world, and it is still building steam locomotives – 50 years after most other countries turned to diesel and electric power because they are much cleaner and more efficient.

75

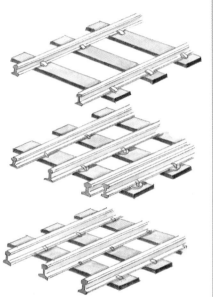

Rails

Ballast

Rail tracks are bolted or clipped onto timber, concrete or steel **sleepers**. These are laid into a **track bed** of hard stones, which is called ballast.

Locomotives ride on two rails, but some electric trains draw their power from a **third rail**, laid between or alongside the normal tracks.

What is a train?

A train is made up of the locomotive (engine) which pulls the rolling stock (passenger carriages or freight wagons). Trains are powered by electricity, diesel or steam engines, and mostly run on steel rails fixed to the ground. Railways are still the most efficient way to carry large numbers of passengers or huge amounts of goods overland.

Steam locomotive

By the 20th century steam locomotives were quite complex machines. Coal from the tender at the rear would be shovelled into the firebox, where it was burned to heat the water in the boiler. This is turned into steam, which was forced at high pressure into the cylinders at the front of the engine. Pistons inside the cylinders are connected to long rods which turn the large driving wheels. The trolley of wheels is called a bogie (see page 87). The buffers at each end of the locomotive and at the end of the railway track help reduce the shock caused upon contact.

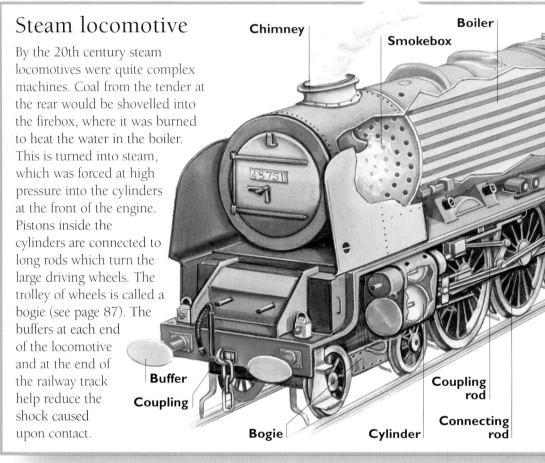

Chimney · Boiler · Smokebox · Buffer · Coupling · Bogie · Cylinder · Connecting rod · Coupling rod

Power source

Diesel power and electricity took over from steam in the 1950s offering more power and easier maintenance. A diesel locomotive has an engine positioned between two driving cabs, while the electric draws power from overhead wires or a third rail, and equipment inside converts this into energy to power the wheels.

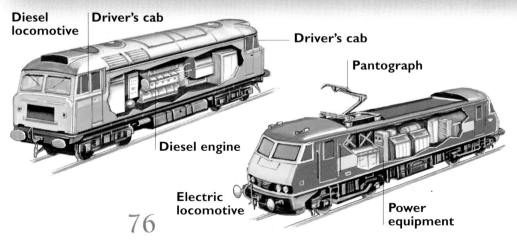

Diesel locomotive · Driver's cab · Driver's cab · Pantograph · Diesel engine · Electric locomotive · Power equipment

Driver's cab

While a train is not steered like a car because it travels on fixed rails, the driver still has to operate several levers to keep it moving. The dials on the dashboard indicate speed, the working of the brakes, how much power is being supplied from the diesel engine or electricity source and alerts the driver to faults with carriage lights and automatic doors.

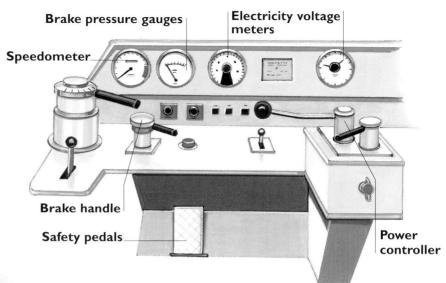

Brake pressure gauges

Electricity voltage meters

Speedometer

Brake handle

Safety pedals

Power controller

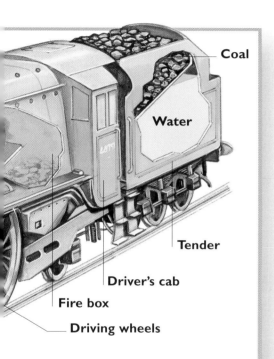

Coal

Water

Tender

Driver's cab

Fire box

Driving wheels

Today, only China, India and South Africa remain as regular users of steam locomotives. They are very expensive to run and need to be taken out of service regularly to clean out the ash and soot.

Types of engine

As well as passenger and freight trains, there are many other types of engines running on the tracks. At nights and weekends, workmen turn out to repair or relay track and check that signals are working properly. Special engineering trains include cranes built on wagons, huge mechanical diggers which clean the ballast (the stones under the track) and ensure the rails are the correct distance apart. Breakdown trains are kept at major depots ready to turn out in an emergency. In winter, snowploughs and snowblowers are placed at the front of locomotives to clear the path for trains to run normally.

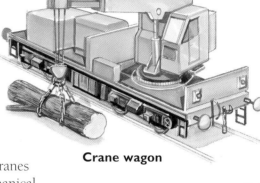

Crane wagon

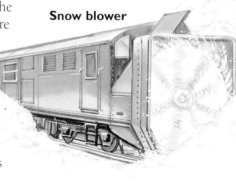

Snow blower

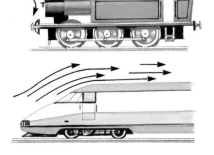

Ballast cleaning train

Wind currents

Aerodynamics

Like sports cars, trains go faster if they are streamlined. In strong head winds, the currents sweep effortlessly over the top of a train with a sloping front instead of being trapped, as happens with locomotives with flat front ends. This does not matter much however with slow-moving local trains or freights.

Running on rails

When rails were first laid in stone quarries and coal mines, horses hauled the wagons. However, the wars against Napoleon of France (1799–1815) left Britain with a shortage of these animals. It was the search for a "mechanical horse" that led to the invention of the steam locomotive. From the late 1820s locomotives were running on tracks in the UK and USA. By 1840, almost 2,400 km (1,500 miles) of railway had been completed in the UK, and in 1869 a golden spike was driven into the final track of the completed US trans-continental railway.

Rocket

Country: UK
Date: 1829
Size: 6 m (20 ft) long
Construction: iron and wood
Top speed: 47 km/h (29 mph)
Number built: 1

Rocket

The Liverpool & Manchester Railway held a competition in 1829 for the best locomotive before it opened in 1830. Robert and George Stephenson's *Rocket* was the winner. It hauled some of the world's very first passenger trains. The design of the *Rocket* also introduced new boiler, exhaust, firebox and simpler drive features which were used in many later steam locomotives.

Locomotion No. 1

George Stephenson designed *Locomotion* for the Stockton & Darlington Railway in 1825. It was the very first engine to have its driving wheels joined together with connecting rods to make sure they turned at the same speed and gave extra grip on slopes.

Country: UK
Date: 1825
Size: 6 m (20 ft) long
Construction: iron and wood
Top speed: 24 km/h (15 mph)
Number built: 1

Locomotion No. 1

Trevithick

The world's first steam locomotive to run on rails was built by British engineer Richard Trevithick for the Coalbrookdale Ironworks in Shropshire. It had flat, tyred wheels, and was so heavy that it broke the cast iron rails. But his basic idea of directing the engine's exhaust steam up a chimney became the standard design.

Trevithick

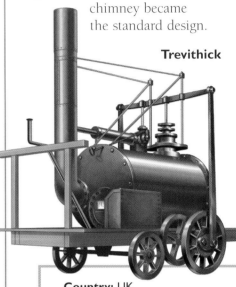

Country: UK
Date: 1803
Size: 4.5 m (15 ft) long
Construction: iron and wood
Top speed: 5 km/h (3 mph)
Number built: 1

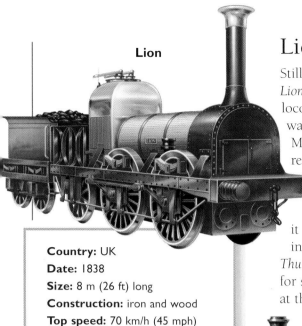

Lion

Lion

Still going strong after 160 years, *Lion* is Britain's oldest working locomotive. This six-wheeler was built for the Liverpool & Manchester Railway, and it was rediscovered in the 1920s being used as a pumping engine. Carefully restored to its original condition, it has been used in feature films, including the comedy *The Titfield Thunderbolt*. *Lion* is brought out for special events, and is kept at the Manchester Museum of Science & Technology.

Country: UK
Date: 1838
Size: 8 m (26 ft) long
Construction: iron and wood
Top speed: 70 km/h (45 mph)
Number built: 2

Stirling No. 1

Patrick Stirling, engineer of the Great Northern Railway from 1866 to 1895, was as concerned about how his locomotives looked as he was about how they performed. His *No. 1* was an express engine for the East Coast Main Line, and its single set of driving wheels were an amazing 2.5 m (8 ft) high. *No. 1* became outclassed as trains got longer and heavier, but survives today as one of the most prized exhibits at the National Railway Museum in York.

Stirling No. 1

Country: UK
Date: 1870
Size: 16 m (51 ft) long
Construction: steel
Top speed: 120 km/h (75 mph)
Number built: 53

Woodburner

Until the 1870s, wood, not coal, was the fuel of steam locomotives in the USA, because it was plentiful and cheap. The wide smokestack could catch the hot embers that might cause track-side fires. The "cow-catcher" was a frame at the front to push cattle off the track.

Woodburner

Country: USA, Canada
Date: 1880
Size: 12 m (40 ft) long
Construction: steel and iron
Top speed: 70 km/h (45 mph)
Number built: over 1,000

Steam-driven trains

Steam locomotives were the dominant form of mass passenger and freight transport throughout the 19th century and the first half of the 20th century. The trains got streamlined and faster – the American *No. 999* was the first to reach 160 km/h (100 mph). They also grew heavier – "Big Boys" had the strength of 7,000 horses and weighed 500 tonnes. But from the 1950s, steam was on the decline.

Snowdon Mountain Railway

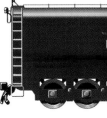

Country: UK
Date: 1896
Size: 8 m (25 ft) long
Construction: steel
Top speed: 30 km/h (20 mph)
On board: 2 crew

Decapod

Country: UK
Date: 1902
Size: 10 m (32 ft) long
Construction: steel
Top speed: 110 km/h (70 mph)
On board: 2 crew

Decapod

As more people had to travel into cities to work, longer and faster trains were needed. The Great Eastern Railway experimented with the *Decapod*, a monster 10-wheeler which could accelerate away rapidly from the station. But only one was built because it was far too heavy to go over bridges safely.

Snowdon Mountain Railway

Rack engines (running on tooth-shape tracks to prevent slipping) began on Mt Washington, USA, in 1869. They are a common sight today in the Alps, and in Wales, where this train made the first steep climb to the summit of Mt Snowdon in 1896.

Pannier

Country: Southern Africa
Date: 1955
Size: 31 m (100 ft) long
Construction: steel
Top speed: 100 km/h (60 mph)
On board: 2 crew

Country: UK
Date: from 1929
Size: 10 m (32 ft) long
Construction: steel
Top speed: 37 km/h (60 mph)
On board: 2 crew

Garratt

The *Garratt* was an odd-looking engine that had the boiler in the middle of the engine, with the tank at the front and the coal tender behind. It works like a modern articulated road lorry – the main frame has a hinge in the middle to allow it to go round tight curves. Over 2,000 were built in Manchester for export all over the world, and many are still in use in Southern Africa today.

Garratt

Pannier

Named after the large water tanks slung over the top of the boiler like a pannier, or rucksack, the *Pannier* replaced a mixed collection of elderly Victorian locomotives. A total of 1,200 were built as local passenger trains, and short distance freights. They were also used as shunting wagons in station yards in the West of England until replaced by diesels.

"Q1" 0-6-0

One of Britain's ugliest steam engines, the sturdy "Q1" 0-6-0 was built during World War II (1939–45) when there was no money to spend on its appearance. All the working parts were easy to reach, and the "Q1" could haul heavy freight over any route. The first "Q1" is still working in the south of England on a preserved railway.

"Q1" 0-6-0

Country: UK
Date: 1942
Size: 17 m (55 ft) long
Construction: steel
Top speed: 45 km/h (70 mph)
On board: 2 crew

Mallard

The all-time world speed record for steam power was achieved by the streamlined *Mallard* on 3 July 1938. The sloping front end was inspired by the *Bugatti* racing car and the train reached a top racing speed of 202 km/h (126 mph). The engine is now in the National Railway Museum in York.

Mallard

MALLARD
4468   L N E R

Country: UK
Date: 1938
Size: 22 m (71 ft) long
Construction: steel
Top speed: 201 km/h (126 mph)
On board: 2 crew

"Big Boy"

The world's largest steam engines were the massive "Big Boys". They were built for the Union Pacific Railroad to haul 4,000-tonne freight trains through the Wasatch Mountains in Utah. They stood 5 m (16 ft) high, and had 24 wheels (16 to drive the train).

Country: USA
Date: from 1941 to 1956
Size: 40 m (131¼ ft) long
Construction: steel
Top speed: 129 km/h (80 mph)
On board: 2 crew

"Big Boy"

PACIFIC   4017

Diesel-powered trains

10000

Because all their working parts are enclosed inside a large steel box, diesel locomotives tend to look the same all over the world and are not as glamorous as steam trains. But they are cleaner, require less servicing or refuelling and can be easily added to, in order to pull the heaviest trans-continental trains. Diesel engines power generators in the locomotive which provide electricity for the special motors that turn the wheels.

Country: UK
Date: 1948
Size: 19 m (61 ft) long
Construction: steel
Top speed: 150 km/h (93 mph)
On board: 2 crew

Burlington Zephyr

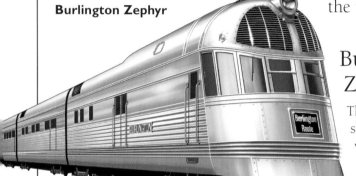

Country: USA
Date: 1934
Size: 60 m (196 ft) long
Construction: steel
Top speed: 167 km/h (104 mph)
On board: 2 crew

Burlington Zephyr

This silver-coloured sleek machine was the world's first diesel-electric streamlined train. It was designed to carry the very rich, and made its Denver-to-Chicago run of 1,600 km (1,000 miles) non-stop in 13 hours. There was only room for 50 passengers in the three vehicles that made up the train because of the equipment inside.

10000

The UK's first main line diesel was built as an experiment to compare its performance against the biggest express steam locomotives. The diesel won easily. Looking like American engines, 10000 and its sister 10001 were coupled together and covered almost 1.6 million km (1 million miles).

Country: USA
Date: 1941
Size: 10 m (33 ft) long
Construction: steel
Top speed: 74 km/h (46 mph)
On board: 2 crew

Deltic

The *Deltics* packed 3,300 horsepower into their small body making them the world's most powerful diesel-electric locomotive in the 1950s. They were chosen by British Railways to speed up its London-Edinburgh expresses. The original locomotive was painted to look like an American engine.

Whitcomb

Whitcomb

Many European countries were desperate for new trains to replace those destroyed during fighting in World War II. American train builder Whitcomb came to the rescue with 200 trains that were so well built, many of them are still working 60 years later. In Italy, they shunt carriages, while in France they are used in factory sidings. Despite their fairly small size, they are both powerful and easy to drive.

Country: UK
Date: 1955
Size: 20 m (66 ft) long
Construction: steel
Top speed: 160 km/h (100 mph)
On board: 2 crew

Deltic

V200

V200

German designers devised this "diesel hydraulic" locomotive that had an automatic gearbox and a complicated series of drive shafts to transfer the power from the engine to turn the wheels. Despite looking smart and being reliable, it was very complicated and expensive to run, and only lasted in service for 20 years. Similar engines ran in Britain too.

Country: Germany
Date: 1953
Size: 15 m (50 ft) long
Construction: steel, aluminium
Top speed: 120 km/h (75 mph)
On board: 2 crew

M62

Russia built over 5,000 of the *M62* diesels for use at home and abroad. However, many of those sent to East European countries have been scrapped because they are worn out and unreliable. Their engines smoked so badly that station staff said they needed to wear gas masks when an *M62* arrived. Also, *M62*s cannot haul passenger coaches in winter because they have no heating equipment.

Country: Russia, Hungary
Date: 1965
Size: 18 m (57 ft) long
Construction: steel
Top speed: 100 km/h (60 mph)
On board: 2 crew

M62

SD40-2

Although it is rather noisy, the *SD40-2* is regarded as the most reliable heavy duty diesel locomotive ever built, and many hundreds can be seen around the world. Colours and marking vary depending on which company owns it. In the USA, their home country, three or four of them are often coupled together to haul freight trains that can be up to several kilometres long.

Country: USA
Date: 1980
Size: 21 m (69 ft) long
Construction: steel
Top speed: 105 km/h (65 mph)
On board: 2 crew

SD40-2

Electric trains

Electric trains are powered from a pantograph (a sprung arm on the roof). It collects the electricity from overhead lines strung up between steel masts along the track, or by a special third rail placed next to the normal track. An electric motor either inside the locomotive or underneath the carriage turns the driving wheels. Trains driven by electricity are more powerful than diesel and steam, and accelerate much faster. Electricity is also a cleaner fuel.

Early electric

Country: UK
Date: from 1904
Size: 16 m (53 ft) long
Construction: steel
Top speed: 145 km/h (90 mph)
On board: 2 crew

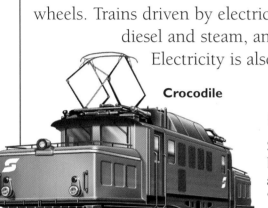
Crocodile

Crocodile

Some of the earliest electric locomotives built for Germany and Austria were nicknamed "Crocodiles" because of their narrow front ends, two cab windows which looked like large eyes and connected driving wheels that looked like gnashing teeth. They were extremely powerful engines, and hauled the heaviest passenger and freight trains for over 60 years.

Country: Austria
Date: 1939
Size: 17 m (27 ft) long
Construction: steel
Top speed: 130 km/h (80 mph)
On board: 2 crew

Early electric

The UK's first electric locomotives were built by the North Eastern Railway to haul coal around the Newcastle area. They only ran for 20 years because they were too complicated and expensive to run. Coal was still very cheap to buy, so the NER went back to steam trains.

GGI

Country: USA
Date: from 1935
Size: 25 m (80 ft) long
Construction: steel
Top speed: 160 km/h (100 mph)
On board: 2 crew

GGI

American railway companies always built things to last, and the streamlined GG1 Class electrics worked for over 50 years. Designed by a Frenchman, they hauled 14 passenger carriages and heavy freights along the eastern seaboard.

Metropolitan

The Metropolitan Railway's line north of London was one of the first to use electric power for its passenger trains. Faster than steam, 20 of these locomotives were built. They were named after famous people such as Florence Nightingale and Sir Christopher Wren. Two of the engines survive in museums.

Metropolitan

Country: UK
Date: from 1904
Size: 12 m (40 ft) long
Construction: steel
Top speed: 105 km/h (65 mph)
On board: 2 crew

CC7102

In March 1955, SNCF (the French Railways) wanted to see just how fast an electric locomotive could safely go. It chose a plain working train (*CC7102*) and another (*BB9004*) for tests. Each train was fitted with a special streamlined front end to improve wind resistance. The engines both reached a still unbeaten record speed of 331.5 km/h (205½ mph).

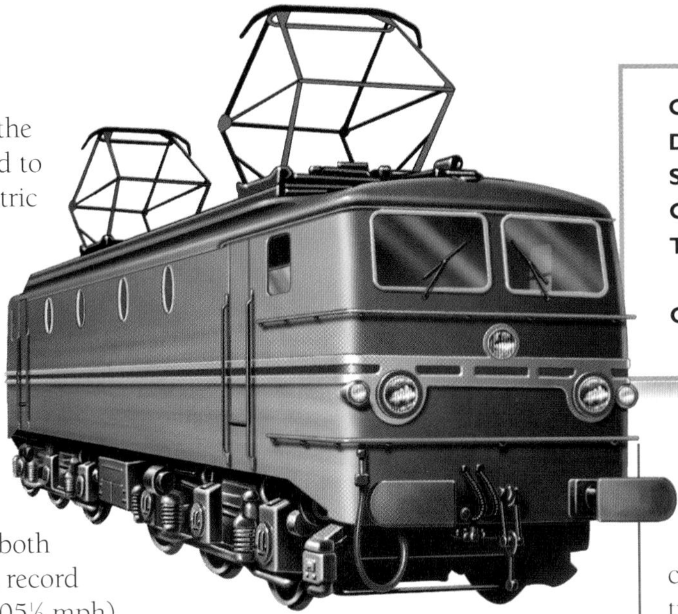

Country: France
Date: 1952
Size: 19 m (62 ft) long
Construction: steel
Top speed: 140 km/h (87 mph)
on standard working models
On board: 2 crew

CC7102

Class 101

The latest German electric locomotives are giants. They can haul 2,500-tonne freight trains at 150 km/h (100 mph), or 14 passenger coaches. It is common for them to travel 1,600 km (1,000 miles) in a single day. The locomotive is filled with computer-controls and can be started in a few seconds. A control centre warns the driver of hazards.

Country: Germany
Date: from 1996
Size: 19 m (62 ft) long
Construction: steel
Top speed: 220 km/h (135 mph)
On board: 2 crew

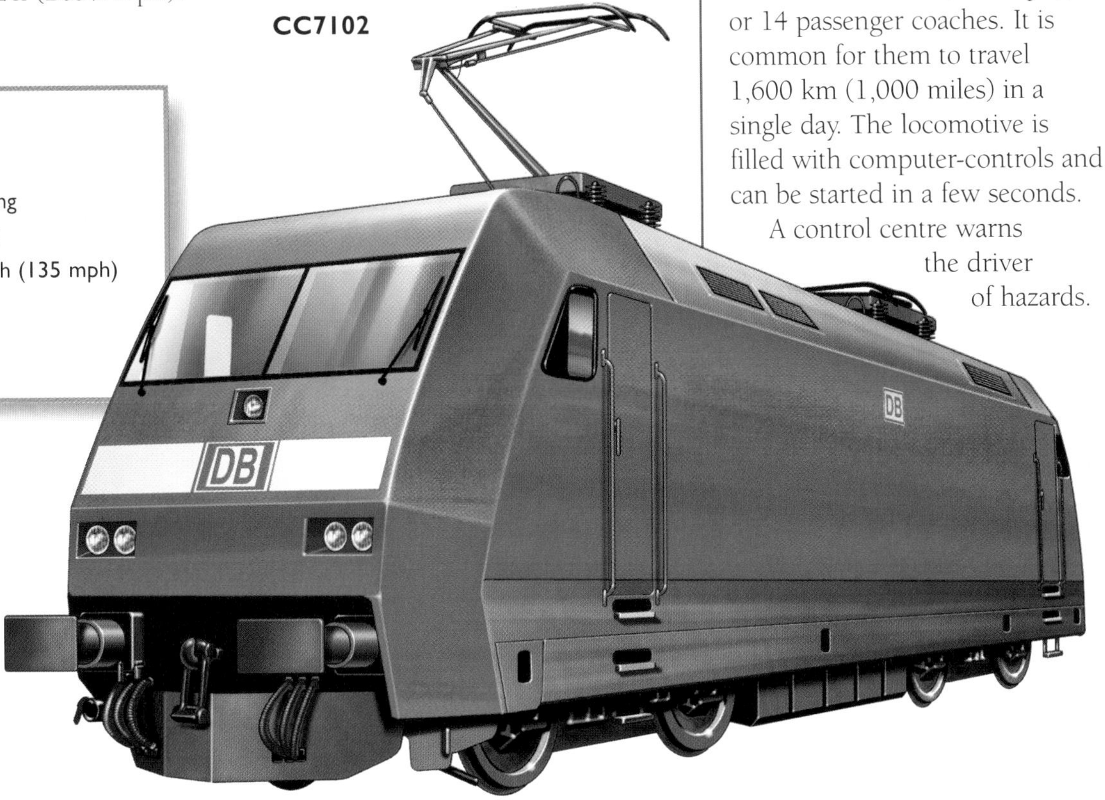

Class 101

Gatwick Express

These new passenger trains are nicknamed "Darth Vaders" because their odd-looking front ends look like something out of a *Star Wars* movie. They carry up to 365 passengers between London's Victoria Station and Gatwick Airport at short intervals. Four coaches in each eight-car train are fitted with electric motors which pick up current from a 750-volt third rail along the normal tracks.

Country: UK
Date: 1999
Size: 160 m (520 ft) long
Construction: steel
Top speed: 160 km/h (100 mph)
On board: 2 crew

Gatwick Express

High-speed trains

High-speed trains are vital for the future of the railways. The *TGV*, *ICE*, *Eurostar*, Japanese *Bullet Train* and other super express trains have won back many passengers who normally travel long distances between major cities by air. Cruising speeds of 250 km/h (155 mph) and higher have cut rail journey times, while improved track, suspension systems and soundproofing give a more comfortable ride. In the next 20 years, trains will regularly run at 500 km/h (300 mph) – 10 times faster than the first trains.

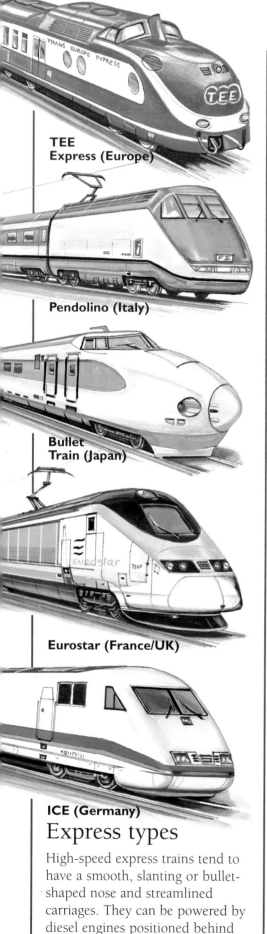

TEE Express (Europe)

Pendolino (Italy)

Bullet Train (Japan)

Eurostar (France/UK)

ICE (Germany)

Express types

High-speed express trains tend to have a smooth, slanting or bullet-shaped nose and streamlined carriages. They can be powered by diesel engines positioned behind the driver's cab, or by electricity drawn from overhead cables.

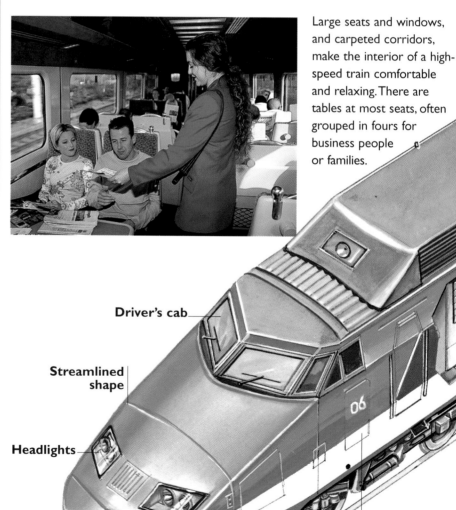

Large seats and windows, and carpeted corridors, make the interior of a high-speed train comfortable and relaxing. There are tables at most seats, often grouped in fours for business people or families.

Driver's cab

Streamlined shape

Headlights

Driver's door

Wheels

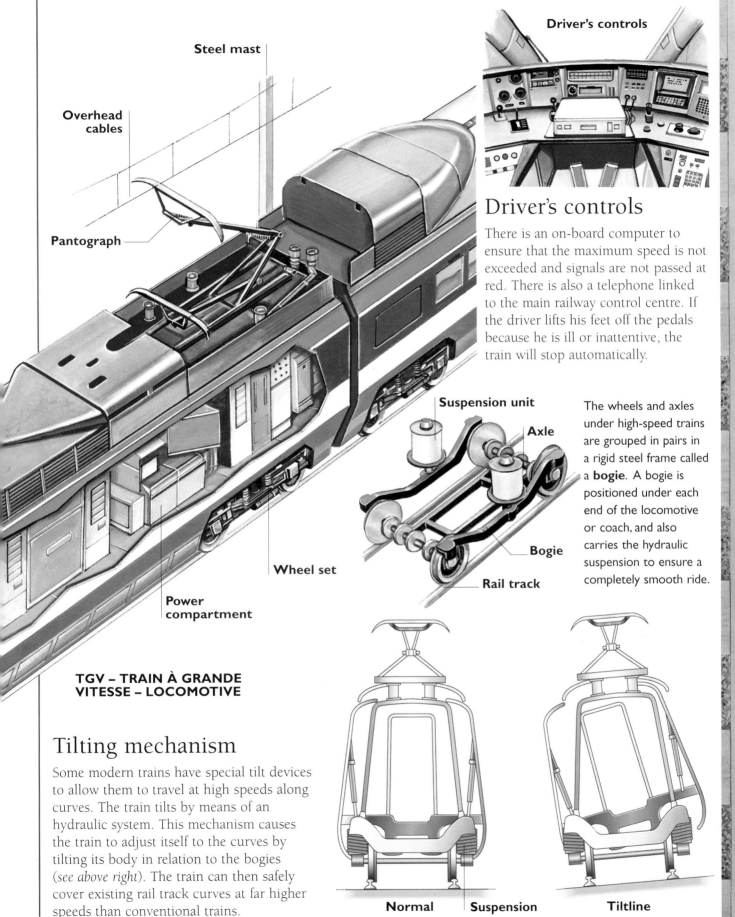

Steel mast

Overhead cables

Pantograph

Power compartment

Wheel set

Driver's controls

Driver's controls

There is an on-board computer to ensure that the maximum speed is not exceeded and signals are not passed at red. There is also a telephone linked to the main railway control centre. If the driver lifts his feet off the pedals because he is ill or inattentive, the train will stop automatically.

Suspension unit

Axle

Bogie

Rail track

The wheels and axles under high-speed trains are grouped in pairs in a rigid steel frame called a **bogie**. A bogie is positioned under each end of the locomotive or coach, and also carries the hydraulic suspension to ensure a completely smooth ride.

TGV – TRAIN À GRANDE VITESSE – LOCOMOTIVE

Tilting mechanism

Some modern trains have special tilt devices to allow them to travel at high speeds along curves. The train tilts by means of an hydraulic system. This mechanism causes the train to adjust itself to the curves by tilting its body in relation to the bogies (*see above right*). The train can then safely cover existing rail track curves at far higher speeds than conventional trains.

Normal   **Suspension**

Tiltline

Around the world on rail

By the end of World War I (1914–18) there were about 1.6 million km (1 million miles) of rail routes, a quarter of which were in the United States. Rail had become the most widely used machine-assisted transport around the world. Great engineering feats of the 20th century, such as the Trans-Siberian Railroad, are still heavily used today, while many modern trains can carry 1,000 passengers or haul thousands of tonnes of freight cargo across continents.

Robinson 2-8-0

Hundreds of these cheap but strong British freight steam engines were exported all over the world to move supplies and soldiers during wars. They were camouflaged to make them harder to spot by enemy planes.

Robinson 2-8-0

Country: UK
Date: 1914
Size: 19 m (62 ft) long
Construction: steel
Top speed: 100 km/h (60 mph)
On board: 2 crew

Country: UK
Date: 1923
Size: 22 m (70 ft) long
Construction: steel
Top speed: 160 km/h (100 mph)
On board: 2 crew

Flying Scotsman

One of the powerful Pacific Class locomotives, *Flying Scotsman* was built to haul the fastest non-stop London-Edinburgh expresses. Water was scooped up from special troughs in the track so it would not have to stop. Over a 40-year period it covered over 4.75 million km (3 million miles). When it was replaced by diesels, the locomotive was rescued from the scrapyard and restored to full working order. It remains one of the most famous locomotives ever built.

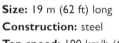

Flying Scotsman

Pullman

American George Mortimer Pullman (1831–97) built luxury passenger coaches that today are known as *Pullmans*. Railway companies paid to use these carriages as early as 1875, and the British *Brighton Belle* electric trains used them until 1972. Many of these hotels-on-wheels have been restored for the *Orient Express* service run by VSOE (Venice Simplon Orient Express).

Pullman

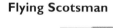

Country: worldwide
Date: 1932
Size: 100 m (320 ft) long
Construction: steel
Top speed: 145 km/h (90 mph)
On board: 152 passengers

Trans Siberian

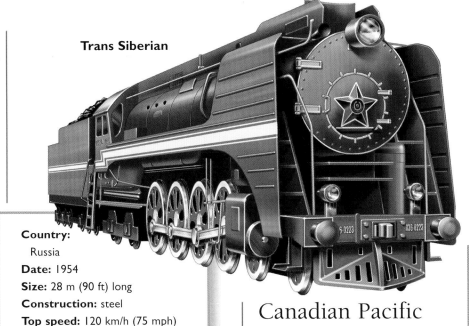

Country:
 Russia
Date: 1954
Size: 28 m (90 ft) long
Construction: steel
Top speed: 120 km/h (75 mph)
On board: 2 crew

Trans-Siberian

The *Trans-Siberian Express* takes nine days to travel the 9,297 km (5,777 miles) between Moscow and Vladivostock, making it the world's longest single train journey. The line was completed in 1905 and was then the world's most northerly track. Today it uses electric, diesel and steam trains.

Country: Canada
Date: 1955
Size: 1,000 m (1,600 ft) long
Construction: steel
Top speed: 100 km/h (65 mph)
On board: 700 passengers

Canadian Pacific

The Canadian Pacific Railway (renamed Canadian National) runs from the east to the west coast of Canada. Passenger trains take three days to cover the 4,634 km (2,880 mile) journey from Montreal to Vancouver. They are often over 20 coaches long, and run past lakes and through prairie country before making the steep climb into the Rocky Mountains.

Canadian Pacific

Blue Train

South Africa has two *Blue Trains* for its 1,600 km (1,000 mile) journey from Pretoria to Cape Town (some also go to Victoria Falls). They have 18 carriages offering the world's most luxurious passenger service with private bedrooms and bathrooms.

Country: South Africa
Date: 1972
Size: 620 m (1,000 ft) long
Construction: steel
Top speed: 80 km/h (50 mph)
On board: 100 passengers

Blue Train

Australian long haul

The Hammersley Iron Company runs trains with up to 210 wagons, each loaded with over 100 tonnes of ore. Three locomotives are needed to get them moving. Along the route is the world's longest continuous stretch of straight track – 478 km (297 miles) across the Australian Nullabor Plain.

Australian long haul

Country: Australia
Date: 1980s
Size: 1 km (½ mile) long
Construction: steel
Top speed: 90 km/h (55 mph)
On board: 2 crew

Carrying goods by rail

In the days before huge articulated lorries, lots of smaller trains carried all sorts of smaller items of goods. Today, goods carried by rail tend to be bulk raw items such as coal or sand in open wagons, or liquefied gas carried in insulated wagons. Large manufactured products such as cars are also commonly transported by freight trains usually on double-tier wagons.

Old style coal wagon

Brake van

Country: UK
Date: 1949
Size: 8 m (27 ft) long
Construction: steel, wood
Top speed: 100 km/h (65 mph)
Number built: 1,250
On board: 1 guard

Brake van

Freight trains used to have brake vans in which the guard sat in a special wooden observation coach coupled to the end of the wagons. His job was to keep an eye on wagons whose brakes were sticking, or even spilling their load.

Merry-go-round

Modern coal-fired power stations are fed by a train named a *merry-go-round* – so called because the train never stops moving. As it travels slowly past the unloading area, a lever opens a door on the bottom of each wagon to release the coal straight onto a conveyor belt and into the furnace.

Country: UK
Date: from 1929
Size: 18 m (60 ft) long
Construction: steel
Top speed: 50 km/h (75 mph)
Number built: 68
On board: 20 sorters

Merry-go-round

Country: UK
Date: 1965
Size: 6 m (20 ft) long
Construction: steel
Top speed: 75 km/h (50 mph)
Number built: over 1,000
On board: 2 crew

Old style coal wagon

The railways once made far more money transporting coal than carrying passengers. Coal was loaded into wagons with simple wooden sides, no roof and primitive brakes. Sometimes 50 wagons were made up into one train.

Country: worldwide
Date: from 1850
Size: 5 m (16 ft) long
Construction: steel, wood
Top speed: 80 km/h (50 mph)
Number built: millions
On board: 0

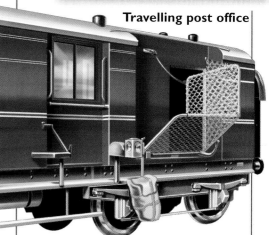

Travelling post office

Travelling post office

Postmen used to travel on mail trains to sort letters and parcels before they arrived at their destination. Bags of mail waiting to be sorted were hung on a large net attached to a steel frame on the side of the track and snatched into the train at high speed.

Car carrier

Brand new cars can be moved by rail direct from the factory to a ship or a showroom in special wagons known as transporters. Up to 100 cars can be moved in one go, often stacked in two tiers. Larger vans and lorries are placed on low trucks to avoid hitting any bridges. Britain alone once had about 20,000 of these carriers.

Country: worldwide
Date: from 1965
Size: 24 m (80 ft) long
Construction: steel
Top speed: 120 km/h (75 mph)
On board: 2 crew

Car carrier

Double stack containers

Double stack containers

There are few bridges on American long-distance railways, so it is possible to stack containers two-high on special flat freight wagons. Powerful diesels can haul trains of up to 2.6 km (1 mile) long, which could mean a half-hour wait at level crossings as they pass through. A crane lifts the container onto a waiting lorry or directly into the hold of a ship.

Country: USA
Date: 1960
Size: 30 m (100 ft)
Construction: steel
Top speed: 100 km/h (60 mph)
On board: 2 crew

Multiple unit

A freight multiple unit train has the engine built into the first and last wagon, so it can be driven from both ends. This saves a lot of time having to uncouple the locomotive every time it arrives at its destination. The middle section is used to carry coal or containers.

Multiple unit

Country: Germany
Date: 2000
Size: 100 m (328 ft) long
Construction: steel
Top speed: 120 km/h (75 mph)
On board: 2 crew

91

Travelling underground

Big cities need public transport to move large numbers of people around, and often this transport is hidden underground to keep travellers away from roads and save valuable building space. Up to 50,000 people can be moved in one direction every hour, at speeds of 16 to 80 km/h (10–50 mph) and often without the delays transport has above ground. Most underground trains are electric and get their power from a third rail. The first underground railway was built in London in 1863.

Country: UK
Date: 1866
Size: 10 m (33 ft) long
Construction: steel
Top speed: 80 km/h (50 mph)
On board: 2 crew

Metropolitan No. 23

Metropolitan No. 23

Although it is now all-electric, the London Underground started with steam. To stop the smoke filling the tunnels and choking the passengers, large pipes were fitted to the side of these locomotives to divert the smoke into water tanks. In the early days, the driver did not have the luxury of a roof over his head. This locomotive can be seen today at the London Transport Museum.

Paris Metro

Country: France
Date: from 1960
Size: 20 m (66 ft) long
Construction: steel, aluminium
Top speed: 55 km/h (35 mph)
On board: 80 per coach

Paris Metro

Over 400 km (260 miles) of rail lines thread their way underneath France's capital city, serving over 450 stations. The trains make very little noise because they are fitted with rubber tyres (making the ride much more comfortable than riding on steel wheels). Over 1,500 million passengers a year ride on the *Paris Metro* with over 4,500 coaches in daily service.

New York subway

With 25 separate lines and 469 stations, the New York subway is one of the busiest in the world. Over 1,000 million people a year buy a subway ticket. Most of the famous old trains, which were noisy, shabby, uncomfortable and plastered with graffiti, are being replaced by new stock.

Country: USA
Date: from 1950
Size: 23 m (75 ft) long
Construction: steel
Top speed: 80 km/h (50 mph)
On board: 80 per coach

New York subway

"Clockwork Orange"

Country: UK
Date: from 1977
Size: 13 m (42 ft) long
Construction: steel
Top speed: 54 km/h (34 mph)
On board: 36 per coach

Country: USA
Date: 1972
Size: 23 m (75 ft) long
Construction: steel
Top speed: 80 km/h (50 mph)
On board: 100

"Clockwork Orange"

Trains on the Glasgow
Underground are nicknamed
"Clockwork Oranges" because
of their bright colour (and
after a well-known novel
and film of the same name).
Formed of several coaches
coupled together, they run in
a circle under the city centre,
going under the River Clyde twice.

San Francisco BART

Hong Kong Metro

Millions of tonnes of earth had to be
moved to make room for the new
fully automatic section of this metro
linking the island city to its modern
Chinese airport. A seven-car
metro leaves the airport
platform every three minutes.

Country: China
Date: 1998
Size: 13 m (42 ft) long
Construction: steel, aluminium
Top speed: 125 km/h (85 mph)
On board: 60 per coach

San Francisco BART

There are 700 fully automatic
BART (Bay Area Rapid Transit)
trains running on special wide
tracks around San Francisco in
California. They have a strange
lop-sided, one-eyed appearance
because the driver only has one
front window. The 5.8-km
(3½-mile) tunnel to Oakland
is the longest underwater rail
tunnel in the USA.

Hong Kong Metro

Guangzhou Metro

Despite being the third largest
city in China, Guangzhou did
not get a metro system until
1998. Space-age trains now
glide alongside gleaming new
skyscrapers and then past the
old-fashioned timber houses.
Although there are only
16 stations at present, there
could be hundreds
before the end of the
decade. The coaches
were built in Berlin,
Germany and sent
to China by ship.

Country: China
Date: 1998
Size: 13 m (42 ft) long
Construction: steel
Top speed: 80 km/h (50 mph)
On board: 100 per coach

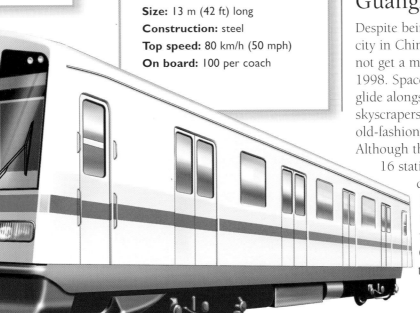

Guangzhou Metro

Light rail

"Light rail" vehicles are simply modern versions of old-fashioned trams. Like metros (see pages 92–93), they can move thousands of people through the streets very quickly. Because they mostly run on electricity, they do not cause the same pollution as cars and buses. While they are expensive to build, they can last five times as long as conventional public transport before they need to be replaced. Fully automatic systems are also more common as with London's Docklands Light Railway.

Old London tram

European tram

Country: UK
Date: from 1900
Size: 11 m (36 ft) long
Construction: steel, wood
Top speed: 50 km/h (30 mph)
On board: 55 passengers

Old London tram

Double-decker trams were once a common sight in cities running on sunken rails: first towed by horses, and later driven by electric power. The driver was often exposed to the rain. The decision to scrap trams after the motor bus became established in the 1920s is now seen as a big mistake, because they were better for the environment than conventional fuel engines.

European tram

There are over 20,000 of these trams on German and other European streets. Power comes from overhead cables laid out in parallel with the rails. The rails have priority over road users and this helps to reduce traffic jams. Also, because no fuel is carried, there is less pollution in city centres. Trams can run for 50 years without replacement, so all in all they offer a welcome alternative means of public transport.

Country: Germany
Date: 1960
Size: 25 m (40 ft) long
Construction: steel
Top speed: 65 km/h (40 mph)
On board: 150+ passengers

New York airtrain

Kennedy Airport's new monorail will cut the journey times into New York city centre from 45 to just 12 minutes. A monorail has a single guideway rail, and the train uses powerful electric motors to speed it along a concrete platform perched on high pillars. The New York airtrains will run without drivers and carry 34,000 passengers a day.

New York airtrain

Country: USA
Date: 2002
Size: 15 m (50 ft)
Construction: steel, aluminium
Top speed: 110 km/h (70 mph)
On board: 100 passengers

Country: Germany
Date: from 1972
Size: 24 m (78 ft) long
Construction: steel
Top speed: 40 km/h
   (25 mph)
On board: 40 passengers

Wuppertal Monorail

Wuppertal Monorail

Although it looks like a fun park ride, the suspended cars rattling under the green girders high above the River Wupper in Germany are used by thousands of people every day. People travelling on this rather special system get a unique view of the towns of Barmen or Elberfield below.

Country: France
Date: from 1983
Size: 26 m (85 ft) long
Construction: steel, aluminium
Top speed: 80 km/h (50 mph)
On board: 50
   passengers

Lille VAL

The French city of Lille was the first in the world to get a fully automatic metro. There is no driver, and, apart from the passengers, the only person on board is the ticket inspector. The electric train wheels have rubber tyres. *VAL* has been so successful that extensions are being built in all directions.

Lille VAL

Country: Germany
Date: from 1995
Size: 25 m (81 ft) long
Construction: steel
Top speed: 100 km/h
   (62 mph)
On board: 75
   passengers

Regio-Sprinter

The *Regio-Sprinter* is one of several trams that can go long distances over normal railway tracks. Powered by a diesel engine instead of electricity it is very cheap to run. The doors are so close to the ground that there is no need to build a special high platform.

Regio-Sprinter

Running on empty

With fuel supplies dwindling and cities getting more polluted from vehicle exhaust emissions, the search is on for forms of transport that use less fossil fuel energy. Car makers have produced "hybrid" cars that run on both electricity and petrol. The power of the sun could offer another solution, and there are already some exciting experimental cars and boats. Future cars may even be powered by hydrogen.

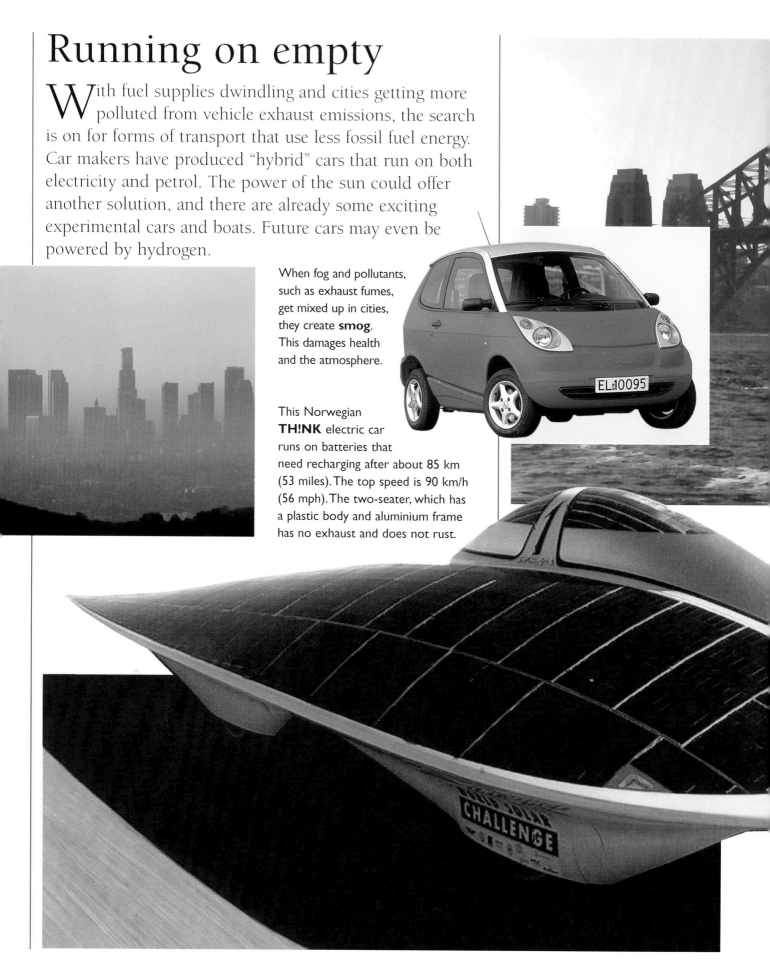

When fog and pollutants, such as exhaust fumes, get mixed up in cities, they create **smog**. This damages health and the atmosphere.

This Norwegian **TH!NK** electric car runs on batteries that need recharging after about 85 km (53 miles). The top speed is 90 km/h (56 mph). The two-seater, which has a plastic body and aluminium frame has no exhaust and does not rust.

This 21-m (68-ft) catamaran, called **Solar Sailor**, combines wind and solar power. It has eight large, winglike solar panels, which also work as sails. It is based in Sydney Harbour where it travels at 20 km/h (12 mph) and can carry up to 110 passengers.

Using strong magnetic forces a **Maglev train** is able to hover a few millimetres above the tracks. There is therefore no friction between the train and the track and this means that the trains can go faster while using less energy. *Maglev* (short for magnetic levitation) trains are being developed in Japan and Germany, where experts predict that they will run at speeds of up to 700 km/h (435 mph).

The fastest solar-powered car in the world is **Honda's Dream**. It can cruise at 90 km/h (56 mph) on solar power, and reach 145 km/h (90 mph) with battery power added. In 1996 it crossed Australia, covering 3,009 km (1,870 miles) in 33 hours and 32 minutes – a record.

In the air

*For thousands of years, people watched the birds'
mastery of the air and dreamed of joining them.
The first people to fly used balloons that blew where
the wind took them. Then, at the beginning of the
20th century, the Wright Brothers learned the secret
of powered flight. These early adventures led to
today's air transport industry and military air forces.*

*Look up into a clear blue sky and you may see a tiny
speck streaking through the air. It is probably an
airliner flying at almost 1,000 km/h (600 mph),
10 kilometres (6 miles) above the Earth. It may
not return to the ground for another
13,000 kilometres (8,000 miles). There are more
types of aircraft flying today than ever
before – from hang-gliders and airships
to airliners and supersonic
research planes.*

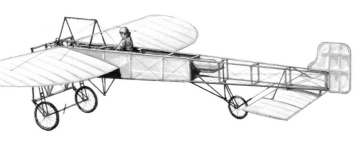

Blériot XI monoplane

A **Boeing 747-400** is nearly 2,000 times
heavier than the **Blériot XI monoplane**
(*above*) which made the first aeroplane
flight across the English Channel in 1909.

What is a plane?

A typical plane has a long slender fuselage (body), with a wing on each side. The tail has a vertical fin and tailplane (horizontal stabiliser). There is an engine in its nose, or two or more engines attached to its wings or mounted on its tail. Wheels may fold up into the nose and wings after take-off.

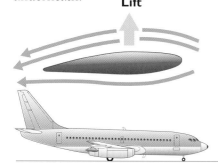

Gossamer Penguin was a solar-powered aircraft designed by Dr Paul MacCready and initially flown by his son, who was 13 and weighed about 36 kg (80 lb). The plane itself only weighed 30 kg (65 lb)! The first test flight was in 1980. The first official flight flown by Janice Brown travelled just over 3 km (2 miles) in 14 minutes and 21 seconds and used solar power directly.

Low pressure

High pressure

Lift

Lift and flight

Planes fly because of the shape of their wings. Air flowing over the curved top speeds up and has a lower pressure than air passing underneath.

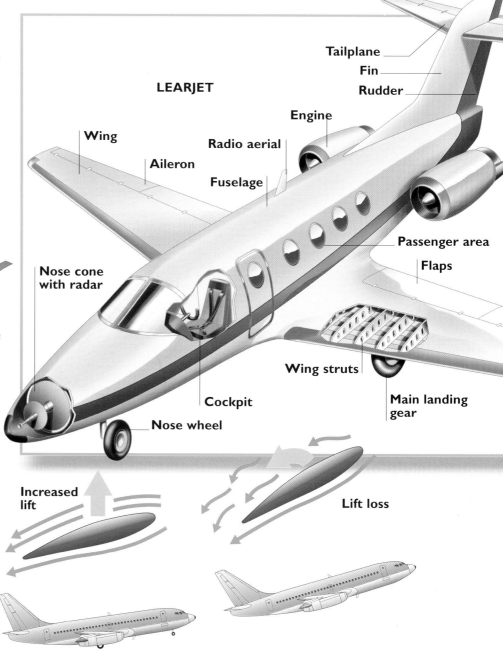

LEARJET

Tailplane

Fin

Rudder

Engine

Wing

Radio aerial

Aileron

Fuselage

Passenger area

Nose cone with radar

Flaps

Wing struts

Cockpit

Main landing gear

Nose wheel

Lift

1. As a plane starts moving, its wings cut through the air and create lift.

Increased lift

2. When its nose tips up and the wings tilt, they create even more lift.

Lift loss

3. But if a wing tilts too much, the air above it breaks up and it loses lift.

The forces of flight

Four forces act on every aeroplane. Engine power thrusts it forwards; air pushing back against it causes drag, trying to slow it down. Wings create lift, which acts upwards, while its weight tries to pull it downwards.

Lift

Drag

Thrust

Weight

Elevator

The parts of a plane

This small plane is powered by two jet engines in its tail. The pilot steers by moving controls that tilt parts of the wings and tail. Ailerons in the wings make the plane roll, the rudder in the fin turns the nose right or left and elevators in the tailplane tip the nose up or down. Flaps assist take-off and landing.

Jet engine

All but the smallest planes are powered by jet engines. These consist of several parts. A spinning fan at the front sucks in air. Some of this air is squashed in a compressor and is heated by burning fuel so that it expands and rushes out of the engine as a fast jet. The jet spins a windmill-like turbine, which drives the fan and compressor. The rest of the air flows around the engine's hot core.

JET ENGINE

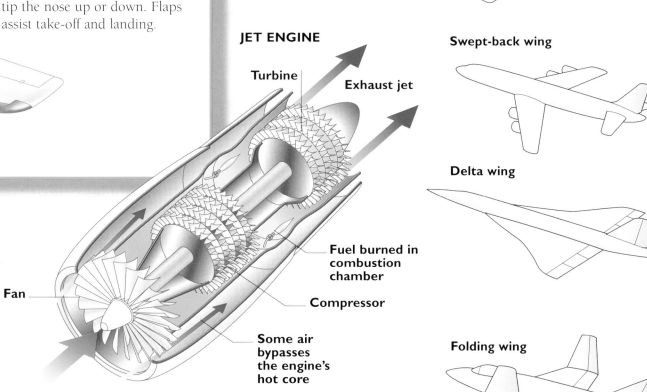

Turbine

Exhaust jet

Fuel burned in combustion chamber

Compressor

Some air bypasses the engine's hot core

Fan

Air sucked in

Types of wings

The slowest aircraft are biplanes and other straight-winged aeroplanes. Faster airliners have swept-back wings. Supersonic aircraft have triangular "delta" or diamond shaped wings. Navy planes have folding wings to fit the most planes in the smallest space. Some planes have turned-up wing-tips, or winglets, to reduce drag and save fuel.

Biplane

Straight wing

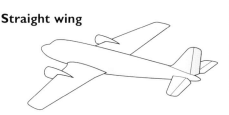

Swept-back wing

Delta wing

Folding wing

The Wright Brothers

Wilbur and Orville

The brothers had a prosperous business selling and manufacturing bicycles in Dayton, Ohio, USA. Wilbur was born in 1867 and died of typhoid fever in Dayton in 1912. Orville, born in Dayton in 1871, lived until 1948. Their interest in flight was inspired by news of Otto Lilienthal's glider flights in Germany in the 1890s.

American brothers Wilbur and Orville Wright made the vital breakthrough in the search for a method of powered flight. They began by building a series of gliders, each improving on the one before. Then they designed the world's first successful powered aeroplane, the 1903 *Wright Flyer*. During this time they also designed and made their own engine and propellers. In 1908, Wilbur Wright took an improved version of the *Flyer* to France and dazzled Europeans with his displays of controlled flying.

In the air!

The world's first controlled, powered aeroplane flight took place on the morning of 17 December 1903, at Kill Devil Hills in North Carolina, USA. At about 10.35 am, a small group of local spectators who had gathered, saw Orville take off, fly into the wind for 12 seconds and land 36 m (118 ft) away. Later the same day, Wilbur made another flight, which lasted 59 seconds and covered a distance of 259 m (850 ft).

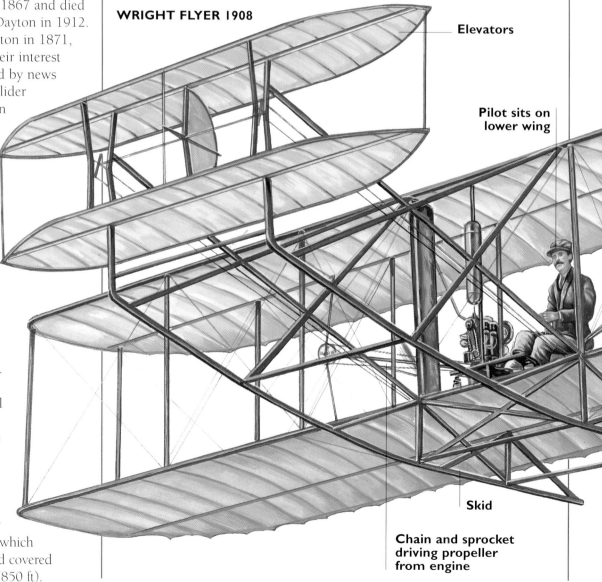

WRIGHT FLYER 1908

Elevators

Pilot sits on lower wing

Skid

Chain and sprocket driving propeller from engine

GLIDER NO. 1

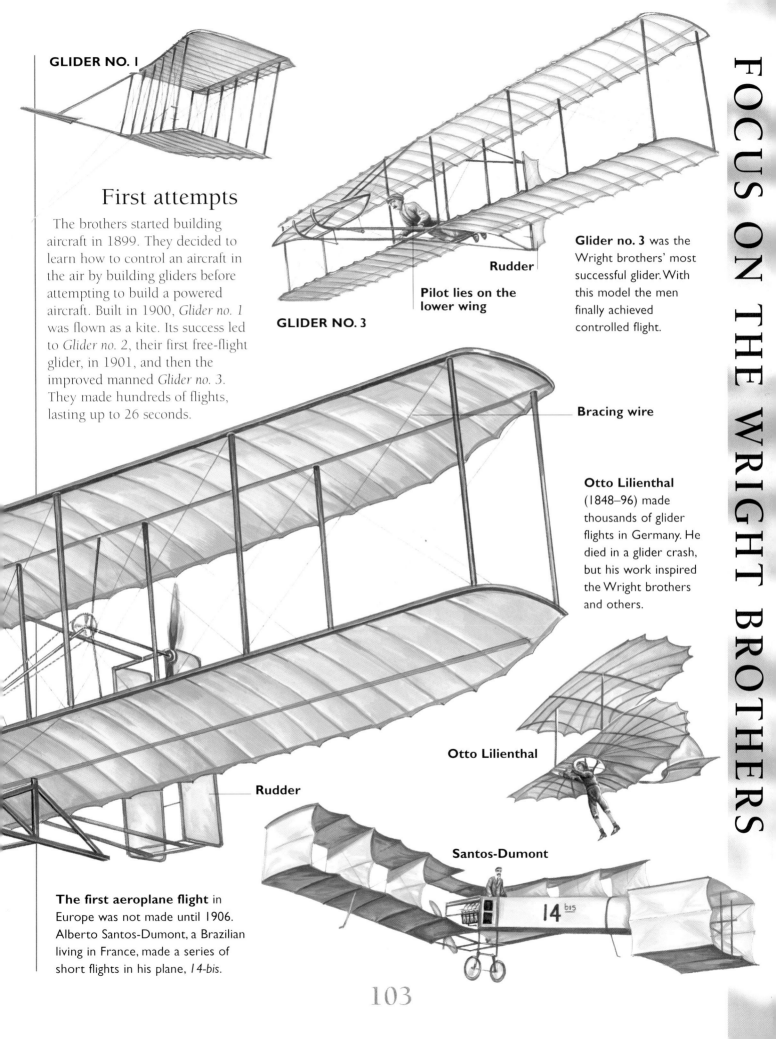

First attempts

The brothers started building aircraft in 1899. They decided to learn how to control an aircraft in the air by building gliders before attempting to build a powered aircraft. Built in 1900, *Glider no. 1* was flown as a kite. Its success led to *Glider no. 2*, their first free-flight glider, in 1901, and then the improved manned *Glider no. 3*. They made hundreds of flights, lasting up to 26 seconds.

Rudder

Pilot lies on the lower wing

GLIDER NO. 3

Glider no. 3 was the Wright brothers' most successful glider. With this model the men finally achieved controlled flight.

Bracing wire

Otto Lilienthal (1848–96) made thousands of glider flights in Germany. He died in a glider crash, but his work inspired the Wright brothers and others.

Otto Lilienthal

Rudder

Santos-Dumont

The first aeroplane flight in Europe was not made until 1906. Alberto Santos-Dumont, a Brazilian living in France, made a series of short flights in his plane, *14-bis*.

Airforce aeroplanes

The first military planes were built during World War I (1914–18). They were flimsy craft – made from a wooden frame covered with fabric and powered by piston engines that drove the propellers. Their main task was to spot artillery. Fighters were built to stop the other side doing such spying. Bombers were designed for attacking targets on the ground, and transport planes for carrying troops and supplies. Military planes today are simply bigger, heavier, all-metal and jet-engined versions of these early craft.

Sopwith Camel

Probably the greatest fighter aircraft of World War 1, the *Sopwith Camel* could twist and turn tightly in air fights. But it could be difficult to control and inexperienced pilots often crashed while learning to fly it. Although known by everyone as the *Sopwith Camel*, it was actually called the *Sopwith F1*. "Camel" was a nickname that came from the hump over the twin machine guns on its nose.

Sopwith Camel

Boeing B-17

Boeing B-17

More than 12,000 *B-17s*, or *Flying Fortresses*, were built during World War II (1939–45). It was a long-range daylight heavy bomber. It could climb to over 10,000 m (33,000 ft) – as high as modern jet airliners – and its fuel tanks could take it 1,700 km (1,100 miles). The *B-17* carried up to 2,700 kg (6,000 lb) of bombs, and was also armed with up to 13 machine guns to fight off attacks from enemy planes.

Country: UK
Date: 1917
Size: 8.5 m (28 ft) wingspan
Construction: wood and fabric
Top speed: 168 km/h (105 mph)
On board: 1

Country: USA
Date: 1935
Size: 32 m (104 ft) wingspan
Construction: armoured alloy
Top speed: 462 km/h (287 mph)
On board: 10

North American Aviation P-51 Mustang

The *P-51 Mustang* was the best all-round fighter of World War II (1939–45). It was a combination of American air frame with a British Rolls-Royce Merlin engine. More than 15,000 *Mustangs* were built during the war. They were armed with six machine guns and carried up to 900 kg (2,000 lb) of bombs and extra fuel tanks.

North American Aviation P-51 Mustang

Country: USA
Date: 1940
Size: 11.3 m (37 ft) wingspan
Construction: lightweight alloy
Top speed: 703 km/h (437 mph)
On board: 1

Boeing B-52 Stratofortress

A giant among bombers, the *B-52* is still in service. It can carry over 22,700 kg (50,000 lb) of bombs and missiles. It has a range of over 16,000 km (10,000 miles) – half way round the world. Remote-controlled machine guns in its tail fight off attacks.

Boeing B-52 Stratofortress

Country: USA
Date: 1952
Size: 56 m (185 ft) wingspan
Construction: armoured alloy
Top speed: 958 km/h (595 mph)
On board: 6

British Aerospace Harrier Jet

The *Harrier* was the first VTOL (vertical take-off and landing) combat plane. Its engine nozzles swivel so that the jets from the engine can be pointed downwards for take-off, and then can be swung backwards for flying. It made its combat debut in the Falklands War (1982), where *Harriers* operated from aircraft carriers and the decks of cargo ships.

British Aerospace Harrier Jet

Country: UK
Date: 1966
Size: 9 m (30 ft) wingspan
Construction: lightweight alloy
Top speed: 1,065 km/h (660 mph)
On board: 1

Country: USA
Date: 1981
Size: 13.5 m (43 ft) wingspan
Construction: alloy and composites
Top speed: 1,040 km/h (645 mph)
On board: 1

F-15 Eagle

This is a long-range fighter that can also be used as a bomber and ground attack aircraft. Its two side-by-side jet engines can power it to two and half times the speed of sound, and it can climb to 18,000 m (60,000 ft).

F-15 Eagle

Country: USA
Date: 1972
Size: 13 m (42 ft) wingspan
Construction: lightweight alloy
Top speed: 2,700 km/h (1,675 mph)
On board: 2

Lockheed F-117 Nighthawk

Better known as the *Stealth Fighter*, the *F-117* attacks ground targets with pin-point accuracy. It uses laser-guided bombs stored in its weapons bays. Its shape and black coating make it almost invisible on enemy radar.

Lockheed F-117 Nighthawk

Airliners

In the 1930s the first propellered airliners flew their passengers slow and low, because piston engines were not very powerful. Flying boats also took wealthy people across continents. From the 1960s jet airliners flew higher and faster, and were affordable for holiday-makers. The biggest airliner is the Boeing *747-400* which can carry 568 passengers. It is flown by a crew of only two, as computers have now replaced the flight engineer.

Boeing 247

Country: USA
Date: 1933
Size: 22.6 m (74 ft) wingspan
Body: lightweight alloy
Top speed: 304 km/h (189 mph)
On board: 2 crew, 10 passengers

Boeing 247

The first modern airliner, the Boeing *247* was a streamlined all-metal plane. It had a retractable undercarriage – wheels that folded up inside it. It was safe and reliable because it could climb and cruise using only one of its two engines. It was designed as a mail-carrying plane, with only 10 seats for passengers.

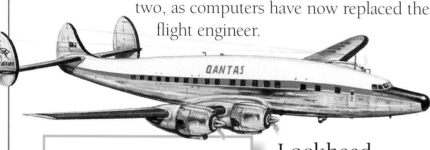

Country: USA
Date: 1943
Size: 37.5 m (123 ft) wingspan
Construction: lightweight alloy
Top speed: 545 km/h (339 mph)
On board: 4 crew, 81 passengers

Lockheed Constellation

Although designed as a long-range airliner, the first Lockheed *Constellations* came off the assembly line during World War II, so they entered service as a military transport plane. This plane's elegant, slender shape and comfortable, pressurised passenger cabin made it popular with airlines and passengers. Larger versions followed in the 1950s.

Douglas DC-3

This airliner looks surprisingly modern for an aeroplane that made its first flight in 1935. More than 13,000 *DC-3s* were built. It was so successful that by 1938 most American air travellers flew in *DC-3s*. It served as a transporter during World War II and returned to airline service after the war. Remarkably, in 1999 about 200 *DC-3s* were still in civil and military service.

De Havilland Comet

Country: UK
Date: 1949
Size: 35 m (115 ft) wingspan
Construction: lightweight alloy
Top speed: 790 km/h (490 mph)
On board: 3 crew, 44 passengers

De Havilland Comet

The *Comet* was the world's first jet airliner. Passengers loved it because it flew higher and faster than any other airliner. However, it suffered a weakness in its metal skin that allowed it to crack. It was completely re-designed and flew again on transatlantic routes as the larger *Comet 4*. But by then Boeing's bigger and faster *707* was flying.

Douglas DC-3

Country: USA
Date: 1935
Size: 29 m (95 ft) wingspan
Construction: lightweight alloy
Top speed: 298 km/h (185 mph)
On board: 2 crew, 21 passengers

Boeing 747-100

Boeing 747-100

The 747 "Jumbo Jet" began as a design for a military transporter, which Boeing changed into an airliner. Powered by four turbofan engines, it was the biggest airliner and the first of a new type, called a wide-bodied jet. The 747's passenger cabin had an an upper deck and a first-class lounge.

Country: USA
Date: 1969
Size: 59.6 m (196 ft) wingspan
Construction: lightweight alloy
Top speed: 1,030 km/h (640 mph)
On board: 3 crew, 490 passengers

BAC/Aerospatiale Concorde

Concorde is the only supersonic airliner: it can fly at Mach 2 (twice the speed of sound). It is 61.7-m (200-ft) long and cruises at 18,000 m (60,000 ft) where the sky above is black, like space. It can fly from London to New York in just three and a half hours. *Concorde* started as two supersonic projects being studied in France and Britain. Although it was a great technical success, its future came into question when an Air France *Concorde* crashed on take-off in Paris in July 2000.

BAC/ Aerospatiale Concorde

Country: UK, France
Date: 1969
Size: 25.6 m (84 ft) wingspan
Construction: lightweight alloy
Top speed: 2,333 km/h
  (1,450 mph)
On board: 3 crew, 144 passengers

Airbus 340

The *A340* is the latest in the series of European Airbus airliners that started with the *A300* in 1972. It is Europe's biggest airliner and the first four-engine Airbus. It also has the longest range of all the Airbuses, 12,225 km (7,600 miles). In 1993 an *A340* set several distance records when it flew around the world from Paris, making only one landing, in New Zealand. It is a rival to the Boeing *747* (*see above*).

Airbus 340

Country: Europe
Date: 1991
Size: 60.3 m (74 ft) wingspan
Construction: lightweight alloy
Top speed: 890 km/h (553 mph)
On board: 2 crew,
  440 passengers

Light aircraft

Light aircraft are small planes with many uses such as pilot training, crop spraying, aerial photography. They are also used for "flying doctors". Most are flown for business and pleasure. A great deal of leisure flying is done in gliders, soaring into the sky on rising air currents. Hang-gliders, where the pilot hangs underneath a kitelike wing, also use these rising "thermals" to stay airborne. Microlights are for one or two people: a three-axis microlight is steered by a control stick and pedals like larger aircraft, while a flexwing is steered by moving a bar attached to the wing.

Blériot Type XI

On 25 July 1909, Frenchman Louis Blériot flew his monoplane 39.4 km (24½ miles) across the English Channel – from Calais to Dover. This first cross-Channel flight took just 36 minutes. His single-wing, separate-tail, engine in-front design set the standard for air transport. Over 100 *XIs* were ordered.

Blériot Type XI

Country: France
Date: 1909
Size: 7.8 m (25 ft) wingspan
Construction: wood with stretched fabric
Top speed: 58 km/h (36 mph)
On board: 1 pilot

Cessna 172

Cessna 172

The Cessna *170* series is the most successful light aircraft. The first *170* flew in 1948, the *172* flew seven years later. These aircraft were used for business and leisure flying, and for training pilots. Many improvements were made with more powerful engines and retractable (folding) landing gear. In 1958, a *172* was flown for 64 days non-stop. Food and fuel were hoisted up from a truck racing down an airport runway!

Country: USA
Date: 1955
Size: 10.9 m (35¾ ft) wingspan
Construction: lightweight alloy
Top speed: 226 km/h (140 mph)
On board: 1 pilot, 3 passengers

Piper PA-28 Cherokee

The Piper *PA-28 Cherokee* was built to compete with the popular Cessna *172*, which it did very successfully. It was used for pilot training, leisure flying and touring all over the world. Piper brought out new models with more powerful engines and better control.

Country: USA
Date: 1960
Size: 10.6 m (35 ft) wingspan
Construction: lightweight alloy
Top speed: 213 km/h (133 mph)
On board: 1 pilot, 3 passengers

Piper PA-28 Cherokee

Learjet

The *Learjet* is the classic business jet. It was named after William P. Lear, who developed the design. The first *Learjet* was an instant success because of its good looks, reasonable price and high speed. Because of its small size, light weight and the power of its twin jet engines, it could climb faster than a fighter. Further versions were built, increasing its range from 2,549 km (1,584 miles) to 5,078 km (3,155 miles) and its passenger-carrying capacity from five to nine.

Learjet

Country: USA
Date: 1963
Size: 10.8 m (35½ ft) wingspan
Construction: lightweight alloy
Top speed: 884 kmh (549 mph)
On board: 2 crew, 5 passengers

Country: UK
Date: 1993
Size: 9.4 m (30¾ ft) wingspan
Construction: composite frame
Top speed: 80 kmh (50 mph)
On board: 1 pilot

Duo Discus Glider

Country: Germany
Date: 1993
Size: 20 m (65½ ft) wingspan
Construction: fibreglass
Top speed: 250 km/h (155 mph)
On board: 2

Duo Discus Glider

From 1985 to 1995 the *Discus* won six world gliding championships. To save weight, its slender body and swept-back wings are made from fibreglass and foam plastic. The slightly larger two-seater *Duo* model is based on this successful single-seater, and is used for training.

Flexwing Microlight

The *Quantum 912 Flexwing* is a weight-shift microlight, steered by moving a bar attached to the wing. It can carry a pilot and passenger with a combined weight of up to 172 kg (375 lb). Fully loaded, it can climb at 365 m (1,200 ft) per minute.

Pegasus Breeze

Flexwing Microlight

Pegasus Breeze

This hang-glider was first developed from a kitelike wing as a NASA project designed by Dr Francis Rogallo to land US spacecraft back on Earth. However, it was never used for that, and instead, was developed for the new sport of hang-gliding. Weighing only 28 kg (61½ lb) it has a semi-rigid wing with material stretched over a frame.

Country: UK
Date: 1995
Size: 10.35 m (34 ft) wingspan
Construction: alloy and composites
Top speed: 140 km/h (88 mph)
On board: 1 to 2

Helicopters

The first helicopter flight was in 1907. It took another 30 years to develop the first practical helicopter, the *Vought-Sikorsky VS-300*, because of formidable technical problems. Once these were solved, helicopters progressed rapidly. Until the 1950s the rotors (blades) of early helicopters were powered by piston engines. Then more powerful turboshaft ("jet"-type) engines became available. From air-sea rescue to police surveillance, helicopters are highly versatile machines.

Sikorsky R-4

Country: USA
Date: 1942
Size: 11.6-m (38-ft) rotors
Construction: fabric and aluminium alloy
Top speed: 131 km/h (81 mph)
On board: 1 crew, 1 passenger

Sikorsky R-4

Sikorsky transformed his experimental *VS-300* (*see below*) into a production model, the *R-4*, by covering it with fabric and giving it an enclosed cockpit. Its simple layout and easy maintenance made it a popular military helicopter.

Country: USA
Date: 1961
Size: 18.3-m (60-ft) rotors
Construction: aluminium alloy
Top speed: 256 km/h (160 mph)
On board: 2 crew, 55 passengers

Breguet-Richet No. 1

Breguet-Richet No. 1

On 29 September 1907, at Douai in France, the *Breguet-Richet No. 1* became the first man-carrying helicopter to leave the ground. The lift was created by four rotors driven by a 50 horsepower Antoinette engine. The ungainly craft was very unstable and had to be steadied by four men with poles.

Country: France
Date: 1907
Size: four 8-m (26¼-ft) rotors
Construction: wood and metal frame
Top speed: zero (hovered only)
On board: 1 crew

CH-47 Chinook

Vought-Sikorsky

Vought-Sikorsky

The modern helicopter, with a large overhead rotor and small tail rotor to balance the twisting effect of the main rotor, was developed in the 1930s by Igor Sikorsky. His *VS-300* lifted off for the first time on 14 September 1939 and made its first untethered flight on 13 May 1940.

Country: USA
Date: 1939
Size: 11.6-m (38-ft) rotors
Construction: tubular metal frame
Top speed: unknown
On board: 1 crew

CH-47 Chinook

The *Chinook* was developed to meet the US Army's need for an all-weather transport helicopter. The current model, the *CH-47D*, can carry 55 troops and 10 tonnes of cargo slung underneath it or 6 tonnes inside.

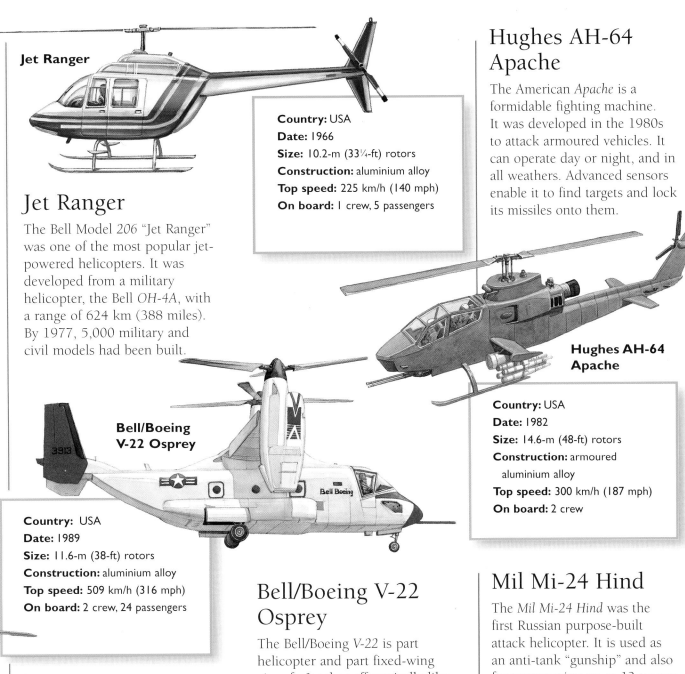

Jet Ranger

Country: USA
Date: 1966
Size: 10.2-m (33¼-ft) rotors
Construction: aluminium alloy
Top speed: 225 km/h (140 mph)
On board: 1 crew, 5 passengers

Jet Ranger

The Bell Model 206 "Jet Ranger" was one of the most popular jet-powered helicopters. It was developed from a military helicopter, the Bell OH-4A, with a range of 624 km (388 miles). By 1977, 5,000 military and civil models had been built.

Hughes AH-64 Apache

The American Apache is a formidable fighting machine. It was developed in the 1980s to attack armoured vehicles. It can operate day or night, and in all weathers. Advanced sensors enable it to find targets and lock its missiles onto them.

Hughes AH-64 Apache

Country: USA
Date: 1982
Size: 14.6-m (48-ft) rotors
Construction: armoured aluminium alloy
Top speed: 300 km/h (187 mph)
On board: 2 crew

Bell/Boeing V-22 Osprey

Country: USA
Date: 1989
Size: 11.6-m (38-ft) rotors
Construction: aluminium alloy
Top speed: 509 km/h (316 mph)
On board: 2 crew, 24 passengers

Bell/Boeing V-22 Osprey

The Bell/Boeing V-22 is part helicopter and part fixed-wing aircraft. It takes off vertically like a helicopter. Then its engines swing forward so that the rotors become propellers. This enables the V-22 to fly faster than any helicopter.

Mil Mi-24 Hind

The Mil Mi-24 Hind was the first Russian purpose-built attack helicopter. It is used as an anti-tank "gunship" and also for transporting up to 12 troops. The two cockpits in the nose are heavily armoured to protect the crew from ground fire.

Country: Russia
Date: 1970
Size: 17.3-m (56¾-ft) rotors
Construction: armoured aluminium alloy
Top speed: 310 km/h (190 mph)
On board: 2 crew, 12 passengers

Mil Mi-24 Hind

Balloons and airships

The first people to fly were carried aloft by nothing more than a balloon, which floated upwards because hot air and hydrogen gas are lighter than the surrounding cold air. Balloons would drift wherever the wind blew them, but by fitting an engine and propeller, steering was possible, and the balloon became a sausage-shaped airship or dirigible. Modern airships are filled with non-flammable helium gas.

Montgolfier Balloon

French brothers, Joseph Michel and Jacques Étienne Montgolfier, made the first manned flight on 21 November 1783. The air in the balloon was heated by a fire of straw. The craft drifted 8 km (5½ miles) across Paris in 25 minutes, and climbed to 450 m (1,500 ft).

Montgolfier Balloon

Country: France
Date: 1783
Size: 15 m (49 ft) across
Construction: fabric
Top speed: 20 km/h (12½ mph)
On board: 2

Giffard Airship

Giffard Airship

The first person to build an aircraft that could be steered (instead of drifting with the wind) was Henri Giffard. He hung a steam engine and propeller underneath a long, thin hydrogen-filled balloon, so that the spinning propeller pushed the craft through the air. In 1852, he flew his airship 27 km (17 miles) from Paris to Trappes.

Country:
France
Date: 1852
Size: 43.9 m (144 ft) long
Construction: fabric
Top speed: 8 km/h (5 mph)
On board: 1

Nulli Secundus

The British Army's first airship was completed in 1907. It was called *Dirigible number 1*, better known as *Nulli Secundus*, meaning "second to none". It was built by US-born British aviator Samuel Franklin Cody.

Nulli Secundus

Country: UK
Date: 1907
Size: 37 m (122 ft) long
Construction: animal skin
Top speed: 32 km/h (20 mph)
On board: 2

ZR-1 Shenandoah

The US Navy's first rigid airship was made from a lightweight metal frame with fabric stretched over it. It was also the first to be filled with helium gas instead of hydrogen, and it carried 22,000 kg (50,000 lb) of fuel and cargo.

Country: USA
Date: 1923
Size: 207 m (680 ft) long
Construction: fabric over alloy frame
Top speed: 130 km/h (81 mph)
On board: 43 (on last flight)

ZR-1 Shenandoah

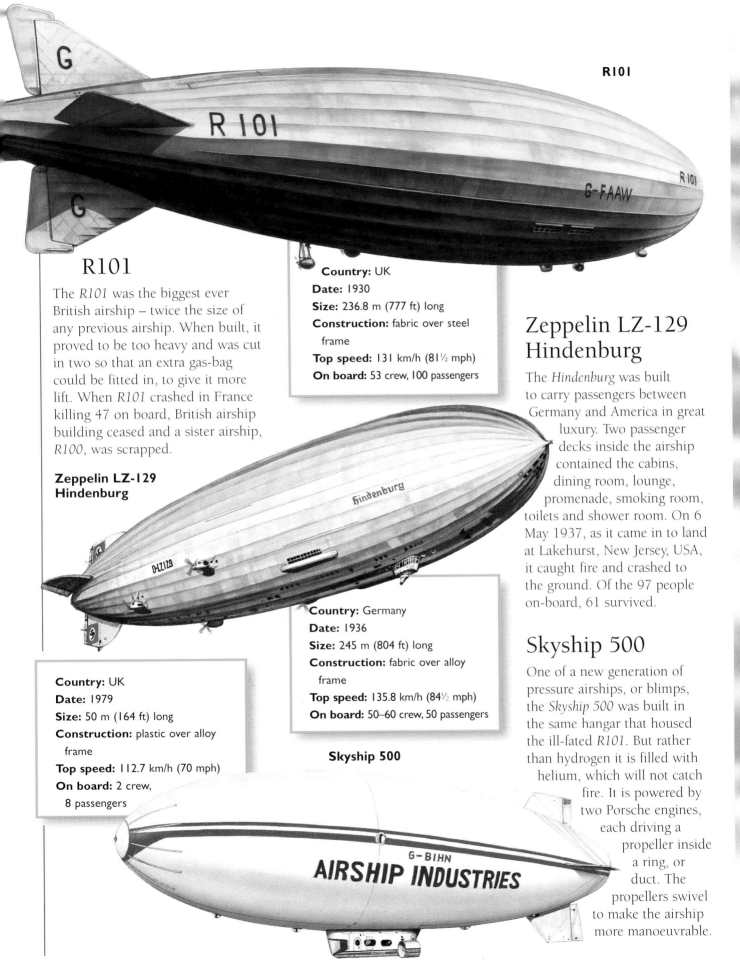

R101

R101

The *R101* was the biggest ever British airship – twice the size of any previous airship. When built, it proved to be too heavy and was cut in two so that an extra gas-bag could be fitted in, to give it more lift. When *R101* crashed in France killing 47 on board, British airship building ceased and a sister airship, *R100*, was scrapped.

Country: UK
Date: 1930
Size: 236.8 m (777 ft) long
Construction: fabric over steel frame
Top speed: 131 km/h (81½ mph)
On board: 53 crew, 100 passengers

Zeppelin LZ-129 Hindenburg

Zeppelin LZ-129 Hindenburg

The *Hindenburg* was built to carry passengers between Germany and America in great luxury. Two passenger decks inside the airship contained the cabins, dining room, lounge, promenade, smoking room, toilets and shower room. On 6 May 1937, as it came in to land at Lakehurst, New Jersey, USA, it caught fire and crashed to the ground. Of the 97 people on-board, 61 survived.

Country: Germany
Date: 1936
Size: 245 m (804 ft) long
Construction: fabric over alloy frame
Top speed: 135.8 km/h (84½ mph)
On board: 50–60 crew, 50 passengers

Skyship 500

Skyship 500

One of a new generation of pressure airships, or blimps, the *Skyship 500* was built in the same hangar that housed the ill-fated *R101*. But rather than hydrogen it is filled with helium, which will not catch fire. It is powered by two Porsche engines, each driving a propeller inside a ring, or duct. The propellers swivel to make the airship more manoeuvrable.

Country: UK
Date: 1979
Size: 50 m (164 ft) long
Construction: plastic over alloy frame
Top speed: 112.7 km/h (70 mph)
On board: 2 crew, 8 passengers

Round-the-world balloons

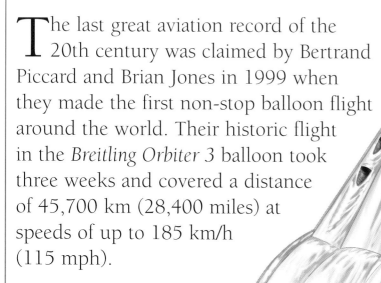

The last great aviation record of the 20th century was claimed by Bertrand Piccard and Brian Jones in 1999 when they made the first non-stop balloon flight around the world. Their historic flight in the *Breitling Orbiter 3* balloon took three weeks and covered a distance of 45,700 km (28,400 miles) at speeds of up to 185 km/h (115 mph).

Tent balloon (helium)

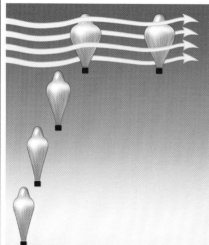

In the jet stream

If a balloon climbs higher than 10,000 m (32,800 ft), it enters a high-speed wind called the jet stream. Air-speeds here can be extremely fast.

Insulating layer

Fire-proof material

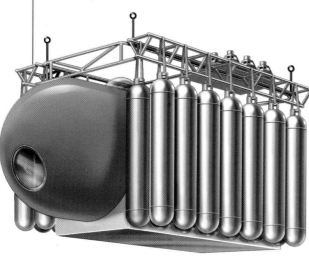

In the capsule *Breitling Orbiter 3* was designed to fly at up to 12,200 m (40,000 ft) above the ground. At that height, the air is too thin to breathe, so the crew flew inside a sealed capsule with its own air supply.

Propane fuel tanks

Hot air rises

Capsule

The *Breitling* balloon was three balloons in one – two helium balloons and a hot-air balloon. The lighter-than-air helium gas reduced the amount of fuel needed for the balloon's gas burners.

Orbiter's route

Breitling Orbiter 3 took off from Château-d'Oex, Switzerland, on 1 March 1999 (*above*). It drifted south-west before finding eastward winds over north Africa. Its route took it over the Middle East, India and China, then out across the Pacific Ocean. It crossed Mexico and set out over the Atlantic Ocean. On 20 March, it crossed the finish line and landed in Egypt the next day.

Piccard Balloon

Designed by Swiss physicist Auguste Piccard, this was the first "teardrop" shaped balloon designed to accommodate the expanding gas that helped it rise. It also featured the first sealed cabin. In May 1931 it became the first balloon to ascend into the stratosphere. Piccard, with Paul Kipfer on board, reached a height of 15,281 m (50,135 ft).

ICO Global Challenger

In December 1998, *ICO Global Challenger* carried Richard Branson, Per Lindstrand and Steve Fossett 19,960 km (12,404 miles) before they had to ditch in the Pacific Ocean near Hawaii.

Solo Spirit 3

Solo Spirit 3, piloted by Steve Fossett, plunged into the Coral Sea on 16 August 1998, when the balloon was torn apart by a thunderstorm. It had flown 22,900 km (14,236 miles). Fossett was rescued from the sea the next day.

115

Traffic watch

In ancient times, when there were few carts on the road or ships on the oceans, traffic looked after itself. The first traffic lights were used in Cleveland, USA, in 1914, and today, our heavy traffic needs even more controlling, to keep it safe and to help it run smoothly. The simple hand signals of a policeman, or a set of coloured traffic lights, are still much in use to keep the roads free of congestion. However, there are also much more modern traffic systems based on computers, satellites and radar systems to prevent air, sea and train accidents.

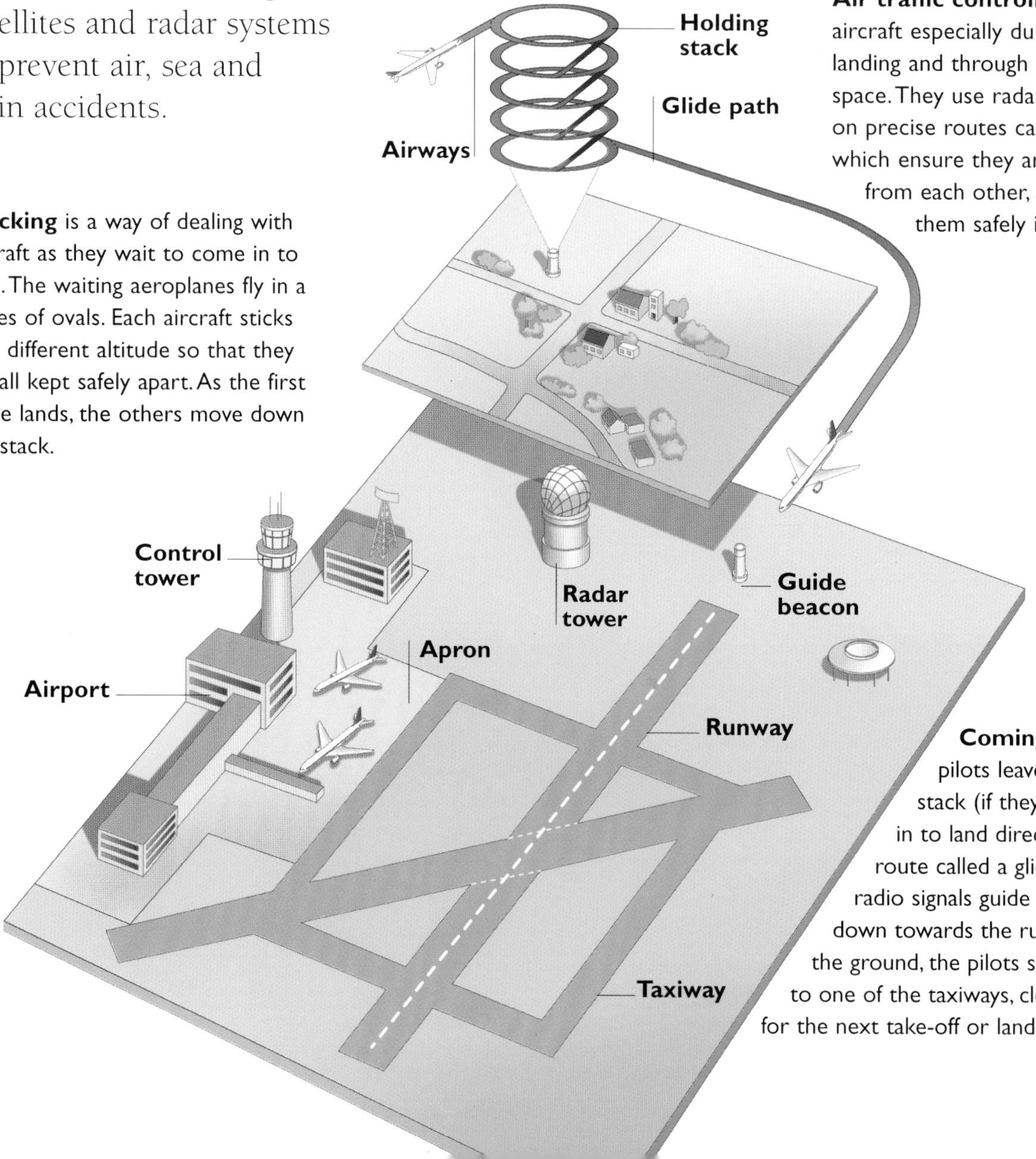

Stacking is a way of dealing with aircraft as they wait to come in to land. The waiting aeroplanes fly in a series of ovals. Each aircraft sticks to a different altitude so that they are all kept safely apart. As the first plane lands, the others move down the stack.

Air traffic controllers guide aircraft especially during take-off and landing and through congested air space. They use radar to keep aircraft on precise routes called airways which ensure they are a safe distance from each other, and to bring them safely in to land.

Holding stack

Glide path

Airways

Control tower

Airport

Apron

Radar tower

Guide beacon

Runway

Taxiway

Coming in to land, pilots leave the holding stack (if they are not coming in to land directly) and follow a route called a glide path, on which radio signals guide the planes safely down towards the runway. Once on the ground, the pilots steer their aircraft to one of the taxiways, clearing the runway for the next take-off or landing.

Railway signal operators use computers to control whole lengths of track and to display each train's position. Signals can be set so drivers will stop if they get too close to another train.

DONT WALK

Tolls are used on many motorways and bridges to pay for the upkeep of those routes. Vehicles stop at a booth where drivers pay to use the road. Traffic can also be counted and monitored through tolls.

Traffic signals may be computer controlled, with sensors to assess the traffic flow and switch the lights to keep vehicles moving. Many traffic lights also have a button for pedestrians to press to cross the road.

Traffic police can respond quickly to any situation, dealing with traffic jams, re-routing cars in emergencies and accidents. This plastic model of a traffic policeman stands on a street in Pusan, South Korea, performing some of the same tasks as a real one.

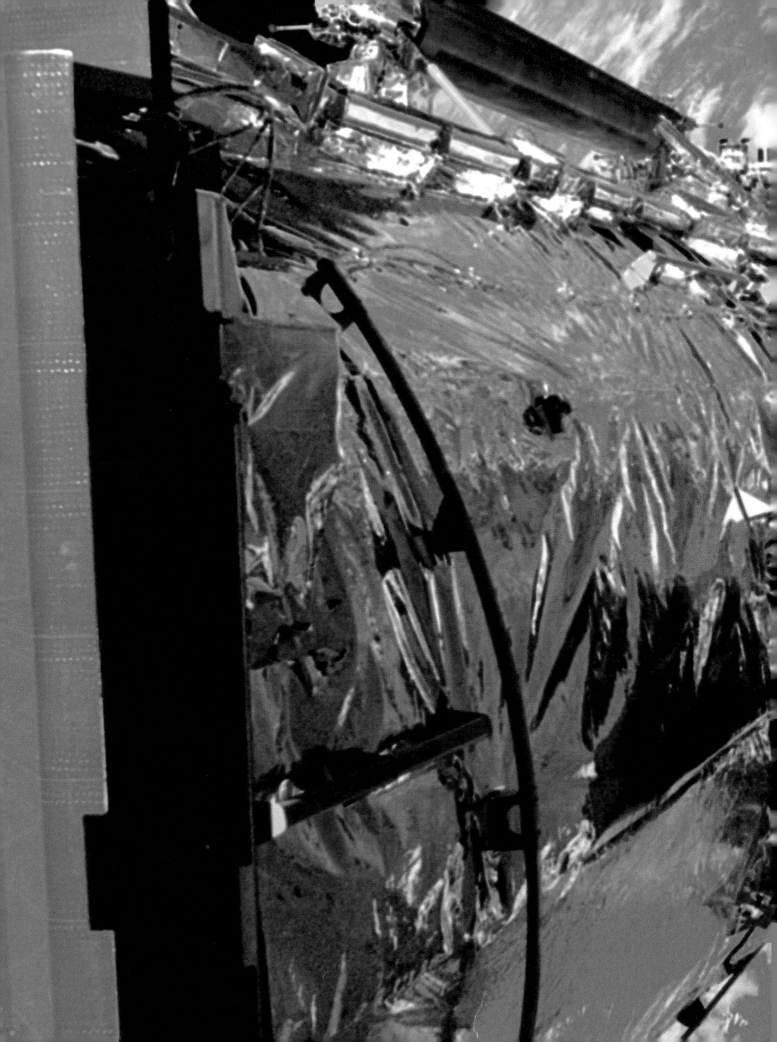

In space

In 1961 Soviet pilot Yuri Gagarin rocketed out of the atmosphere in his Vostok capsule and orbited the Earth. His historic flight marked the beginning of manned space flight. Since then, unmanned spacecraft have explored the solar system and people have lived in space stations and landed on the Moon. Now, space shuttles ferry people into Earth's orbit and back.

Space flight is the youngest of all the different forms of transport, so it is not available to all of us – yet. But, just as aeroplanes were once flown only by a small group of intrepid pioneers and now carry millions of passengers each year, "space planes" may one day be an equally popular transport .

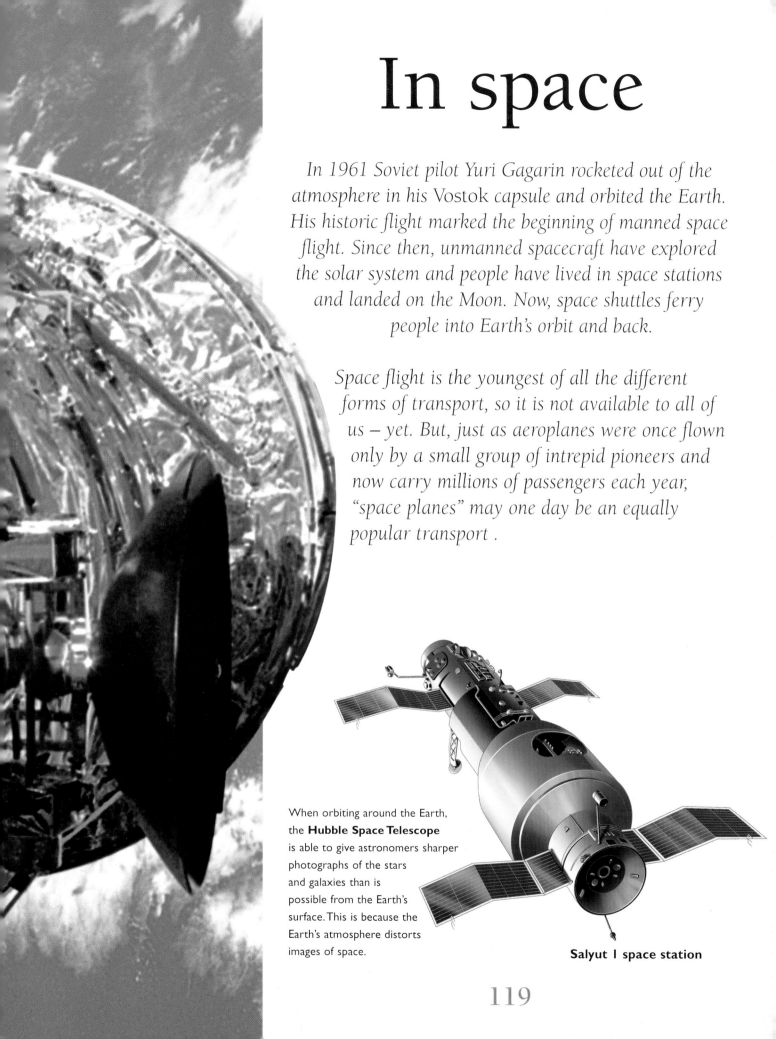

When orbiting around the Earth, the **Hubble Space Telescope** is able to give astronomers sharper photographs of the stars and galaxies than is possible from the Earth's surface. This is because the Earth's atmosphere distorts images of space.

Salyut I space station

What is a spacecraft?

Spacecraft are vehicles designed to travel in space. They include satellites orbiting the Earth, probes sent to the planets and manned vehicles such as the American *Space Shuttle* and Russian *Soyuz* craft. They are launched by immensely powerful rockets. In space, they steer by firing smaller thrusters.

Robert H. Goddard, an American scientist, launched the first liquid-fuel rocket at Auburn, Massachusetts, USA, on 16 March 1926. It flew 56 m (184 ft) in 2.5 seconds.

The German **V-2** was the first successful modern rocket. It stood 14 m (56 ft) high and weighed 12,500 kg (27,500 lb).

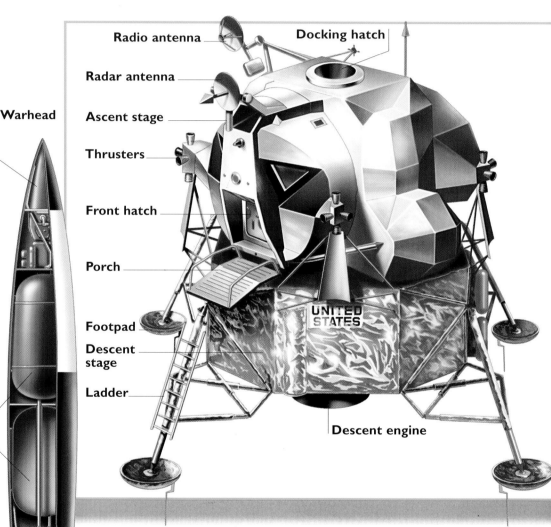

Warhead

Alcohol fuel tank

Liquid oxygen tank

Radio antenna
Docking hatch
Radar antenna
Ascent stage
Thrusters
Front hatch
Porch
Footpad
Descent stage
Ladder
Descent engine

UNITED STATES

V-2 rocket

German scientists and engineers developed the *V-2* rocket weapon during World War II (1939–45). It carried a 1,000 kg (2,200 lb) warhead a distance of 275 km (171 miles), faster than the speed of sound.

Spacecraft

All spacecraft need electricity to power their instruments and communications equipment. Most spacecraft make electricity from sunlight by using solar panels. Beyond the orbit of Mars, there is too little sunlight for solar panels to work, so space probes going to the outer planets use nuclear generators. American manned spacecraft use fuel cells to make electricity from a chemical reaction between hydrogen and oxygen.

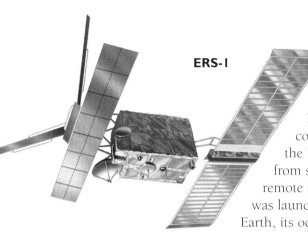

ERS-1

Remote sensing

Remote sensing satellites collect information about the Earth or another planet from space. The European remote sensing satellite (*ERS-1*) was launched in 1991 to study the Earth, its oceans and atmosphere.

Spacecraft anatomy

The *Apollo Lunar Excursion Module* (*LEM*) could land two astronauts on the Moon. It was a very unusual spacecraft. The base, or descent stage, had a rocket engine to slow down the *LEM* for landing. Then, at the end of the mission, the *LEM* split in two and the descent stage formed a launch-pad for the upper part, or ascent stage. It steered by firing thrusters arranged in groups of four. Broad foot pads ensured that it did not sink into the Moon's surface.

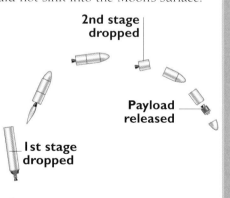

2nd stage dropped

Payload released

1st stage dropped

Rocket types

Rockets like the European *Ariane* launcher, burn liquid fuel. *Ariane's* liquid engines are assisted by two strap-on solid propellant engines. Burning requires oxygen, so the fuel is mixed with a liquid called an oxidiser that provides the oxygen. Liquid fuel rocket engines are controllable. They can be turned on and off, and varied in power, by pumping more or less fuel into the engine. Another type of rocket burns solid propellant, a mixture of solid fuel and oxidiser. Once lit, it burns until no propellant is left.

Payload

3rd stage

2nd stage

Propellant

Oxidiser

1st stage

Booster rocket

ARIANE

SOLID ROCKET BOOSTER

Rocket launch

A rocket is actually several rockets, called stages, stacked on top of each other. Each stage falls away as it runs out of fuel.

Booster dropped

Lift off

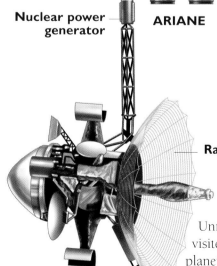

Nuclear power generator

Radio dish

GALILEO

Space probes

Unmanned space probes have visited and studied most of the planets and many of their moons. The *Galileo* probe, launched in 1989, studied Jupiter and its moons in the 1990s.

121

Satellites and probes

The Space Age began on 4 October 1957, when Russia sent the first man-made object into orbit. It was called *Sputnik*, (meaning "traveller"). Other unmanned spacecraft were launched to explore the solar system. They landed on the Moon, photographed the planets, mapped Venus and looked for life on Mars. Today, satellites orbit the Earth to monitor the weather and others study the universe with telescopes. Probes have visited Jupiter and the outer planets, acting as the robot eyes and ears of scientists and astronauts who may follow them one day.

Sputnik-1

A metal ball with a radio transmitter, *Sputnik-1* had four long aerials to send its bleeps to an amazed world. Its launch sparked a "space race" between the USA and Russia that lasted until *Apollo 11* in 1969.

Sputnik-1

Country: Russia
Date: 1957
Size: 58 cm (2 ft) across
Construction: metal sphere
Top speed: 28,000 km/h (17,500 mph)

Surveyor 3

Landing on a part of the Moon called the Ocean of Storms, *Surveyor 3* took 6,315 photographs of the Moon's surface. It dug a small trench in the ground to test the Moon's strength in preparation for later manned landings. In 1969, *Apollo 12* landed near the craft and astronauts brought parts of the *Surveyor* back to Earth.

Surveyor 3

Country: USA
Date: 1967
Size: 3 m (10 ft) high
Construction: lightweight alloys
Top speed: 39,000 km/h (24,230 mph)

Viking

In 1976, two *Viking* spacecraft went into orbit around the planet Mars. They dropped probes onto the surface. The landers carried a chemical laboratory, a weather station that sent daily reports until 1983, and an instrument to study Mars-quakes. They took thousands of photographs, and also tested samples of the rust-red soil for signs of life on Mars. No life forms were detected.

Viking

Country: USA
Date: 1976
Size: 3 m (9¾ ft)
Construction: lightweight alloys
Top speed: 39,000 km/h (24,230 mph)

Voyager

The first close-up images and measurements of distant planets were taken by Voyager. New moons and rings around Jupiter were revealed. The instruments ran on nuclear power, and a radio dish 3.7 m (12 ft) across kept the probe in contact with Earth.

Voyager

Country: USA
Date: 1977
Size: 3 m (9¾ ft) high
Construction: aluminium
Top speed: 52,000 km/h (32,000 mph)

Country: USA
Date: 1989
Size: 5.3 m (17½ ft) high
Construction: lightweight alloys
Top speed: 86,760 km/h (54,225 mph)

Galileo

In 1995, *Galileo* became the first spacecraft to orbit Jupiter. It was named after the great Italian scientist, Galileo Galilei, who discovered four of Jupiter's moons. A small probe was dropped into Jupiter's atmosphere. This sent back measurements for 57 minutes until it was destroyed by heat and crushing pressure.

Galileo

Hubble Space Telescope

This orbiting telescope has given astronomers amazing pictures of stars forming and exploding with no interference from the Earth's atmosphere. But the first images were blurred because a mistake had been made when making the telescope's main mirror. Space Shuttle astronauts repaired the telescope using the Canadarm.

Hubble Space Telescope

Country: USA
Date: 1990
Size: 13.3 m (43½ ft) long
Construction: lightweight alloys
Top speed: 28,000 km/h (17,500 mph)

Cassini-Huygens

The largest space probe ever launched, *Cassini-Huygens* is two space probes in one. The main craft, *Cassini*, will study the ringed planet Saturn in 2004. It carries *Huygens*, a smaller probe which it will drop on to Saturn's largest moon, Titan. If *Huygens* survives the landing, it will test whether the surface is solid or liquid.

Cassini-Huygens

Country: USA, Europe
Date: 1997
Size: 6.8 m (22¼ ft) high
Construction: lightweight alloys
Top speed: 68,400 km/h (42,511 mph)

Taking man to the Moon

A new age in exploration and transport began when Russian cosmonaut Yuri Gagarin became the first person to be launched into space. He made one orbit in his tiny capsule and returned safely to Earth. Not to be outdone, America launched its own series of manned spaceflights to learn how to control spacecraft and link them together. The "space race" was on and was "won" by the *Apollo* spacecraft landing 12 astronauts on the Moon between 1969 and 1972.

Mercury Redstone 3

Country: Russia
Date: 1961
Size: 2.3m (7½ ft)
Construction:
  lightweight alloys
Top speed: 28,000 km/h
  (17,500 mph)
On board: 1

Vostok 1

Mercury Redstone 3

The first American astronaut in space was Alan Shepard on board *Mercury Redstone 3* (MR-3). A *Redstone* rocket boosted his capsule *Freedom 7* to a height of 187.5 km (116½ miles). There was not enough power to place the capsule in orbit, so it re-entered the atmosphere and fell back to Earth.

Country: USA
Date: 1961
Size: 2.9 m (9½ ft)
Construction: lightweight alloys
Top speed: 8,336 km/h
  (5,180 mph)
On board: 1

Gemini 6

Twice the size and weight of *Mercury,* the *Gemini* spacecraft carried a two-man crew. There were 10 *Gemini* flights in less than two years. *Gemini 6* was to be launched to manoeuvre close to a rocket already in space. But the rocket was lost, and *Gemini 6* was delayed a few months so that it could use *Gemini 7* as its target instead. *Gemini 6*, flown by Wally Schirra and Thomas Stafford, came within 0.3 m (¼ ft) of *Gemini 7*.

Mercury Atlas MA-6

John Glenn was the first American astronaut to orbit the Earth. His Mercury capsule, *Friendship 7*, was launched by an *Atlas* rocket (more powerful than the *Redstone* rockets on the early *Mercury* flights). After three orbits when it seemed that the capsule's heat shield had come loose, Glenn's flight was cut short for fear it would burn up on re-entering the atmosphere. But Glenn landed safely.

Mercury Atlas MA-6

Country: USA
Date: 1962
Size: 2.9 m (9½ ft)
Construction: lightweight alloys
Top speed: 28,234 km/h
  (17,543 mph)
On board: 1

Vostok 1

The *Vostok* (meaning "east" in Russian) *1* space capsule was a hollow metal ball just big enough for Yuri Gagarin to lie down inside for the flight lasting 1 hour 48 minutes. It was completely covered with heat shield material to protect him from the intense heat of re-entering the atmosphere. A rocket engine on the capsule was fired after one orbit to slow the capsule and make it fall back to Earth.

Country: USA
Date: 1965
Size: 5.6 m (18½ ft)
Body: lightweight alloys
Top speed: 28,000 km/h
  (17,500 mph)
On board: 2

Gemini 6

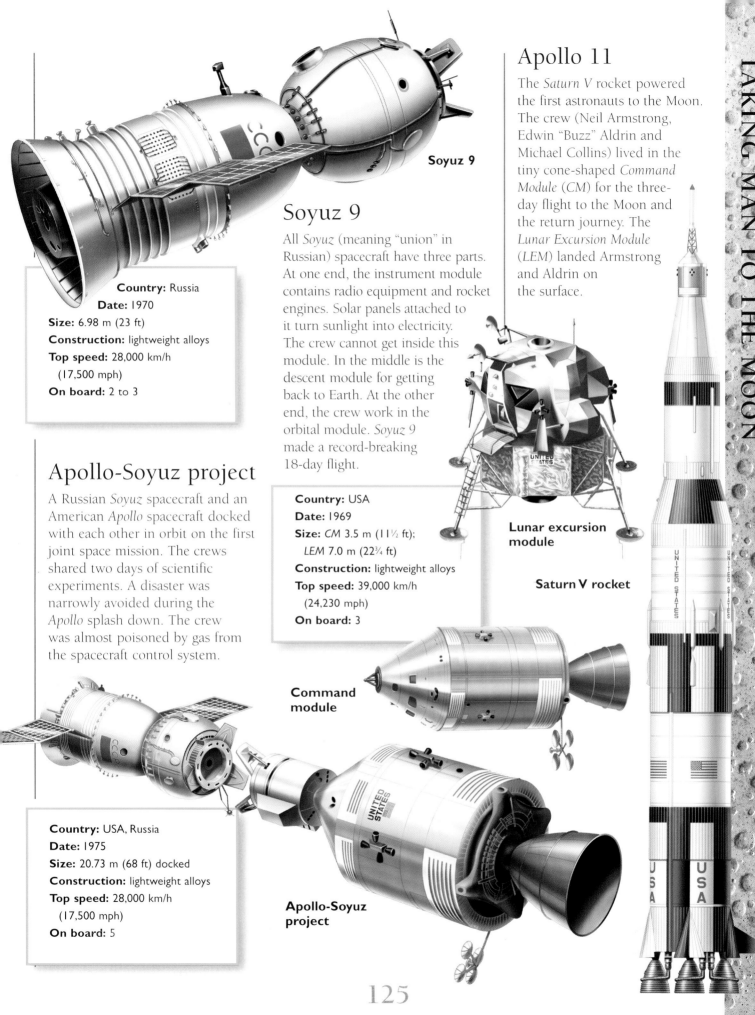

Soyuz 9

Country: Russia
Date: 1970
Size: 6.98 m (23 ft)
Construction: lightweight alloys
Top speed: 28,000 km/h
(17,500 mph)
On board: 2 to 3

Soyuz 9

All *Soyuz* (meaning "union" in Russian) spacecraft have three parts. At one end, the instrument module contains radio equipment and rocket engines. Solar panels attached to it turn sunlight into electricity. The crew cannot get inside this module. In the middle is the descent module for getting back to Earth. At the other end, the crew work in the orbital module. *Soyuz 9* made a record-breaking 18-day flight.

Apollo-Soyuz project

A Russian *Soyuz* spacecraft and an American *Apollo* spacecraft docked with each other in orbit on the first joint space mission. The crews shared two days of scientific experiments. A disaster was narrowly avoided during the *Apollo* splash down. The crew was almost poisoned by gas from the spacecraft control system.

Country: USA
Date: 1969
Size: CM 3.5 m (11½ ft);
LEM 7.0 m (22¾ ft)
Construction: lightweight alloys
Top speed: 39,000 km/h
(24,230 mph)
On board: 3

Apollo 11

The *Saturn V* rocket powered the first astronauts to the Moon. The crew (Neil Armstrong, Edwin "Buzz" Aldrin and Michael Collins) lived in the tiny cone-shaped *Command Module* (CM) for the three-day flight to the Moon and the return journey. The *Lunar Excursion Module* (LEM) landed Armstrong and Aldrin on the surface.

Lunar excursion module

Saturn V rocket

Command module

Country: USA, Russia
Date: 1975
Size: 20.73 m (68 ft) docked
Construction: lightweight alloys
Top speed: 28,000 km/h
(17,500 mph)
On board: 5

Apollo-Soyuz project

125

The space shuttle

The space shuttle is the first reusable spacecraft. It blasts off like a rocket and lands again like an airliner on a runway. Within 14 days it can be ready for another flight. Its main job is to carry satellites, experiments and parts of the planned international space station into orbit. The immense thrust needed to launch the winged craft, which is called the orbiter, is supplied by three main engines in its tail, fed with fuel from an external tank and two solid rocket boosters.

A **space shuttle** launch is a spectacular sight. As space shuttle *Endeavour* takes off (*above*), searing hot gases at 3,000°C (5,400°F) race out of the orbiter's engines and its rocket boosters at 10,000 km/h (620 mph).

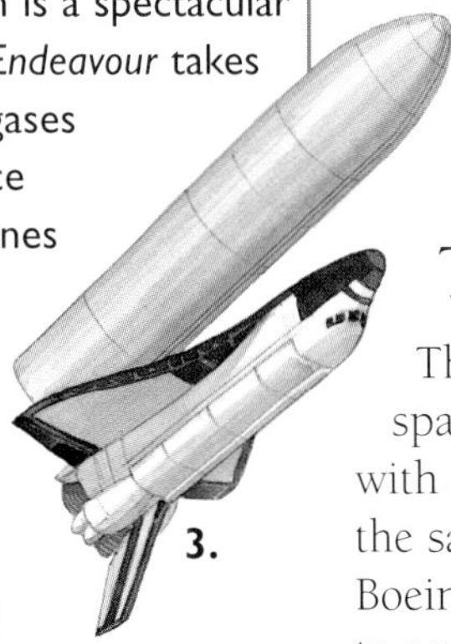

The orbiter

The orbiter is the space-plane of the space shuttle: it is 37 m (120 ft) long with a wingspan of 24 m (79 ft) – about the same size as a small airliner like the Boeing 737. It can carry a crew of up to seven into Earth's orbit.

3.

2.

The launch

The shuttle blasts off using the orbiter's main engines and two solid rocket boosters (**1**). Two minutes later, at a height of 45 km (28 miles), the boosters fall away (**2**). They land in the Atlantic Ocean by parachute. Ships collect them so that they can be refuelled for another flight. At a height of 113 km (70 miles), 8.5 minutes into the mission, the almost empty external tank (**3**) falls into the Indian Ocean.

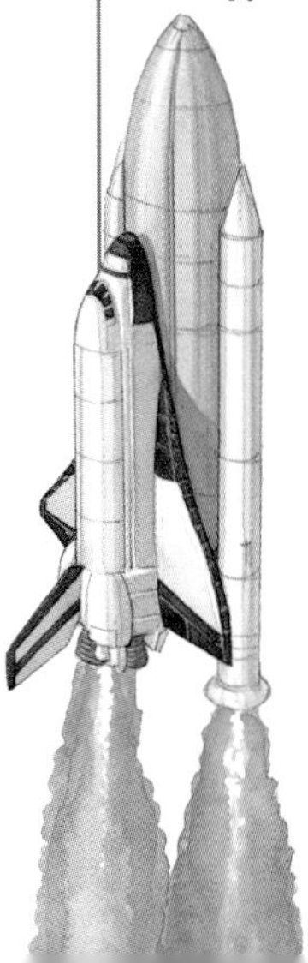

1.

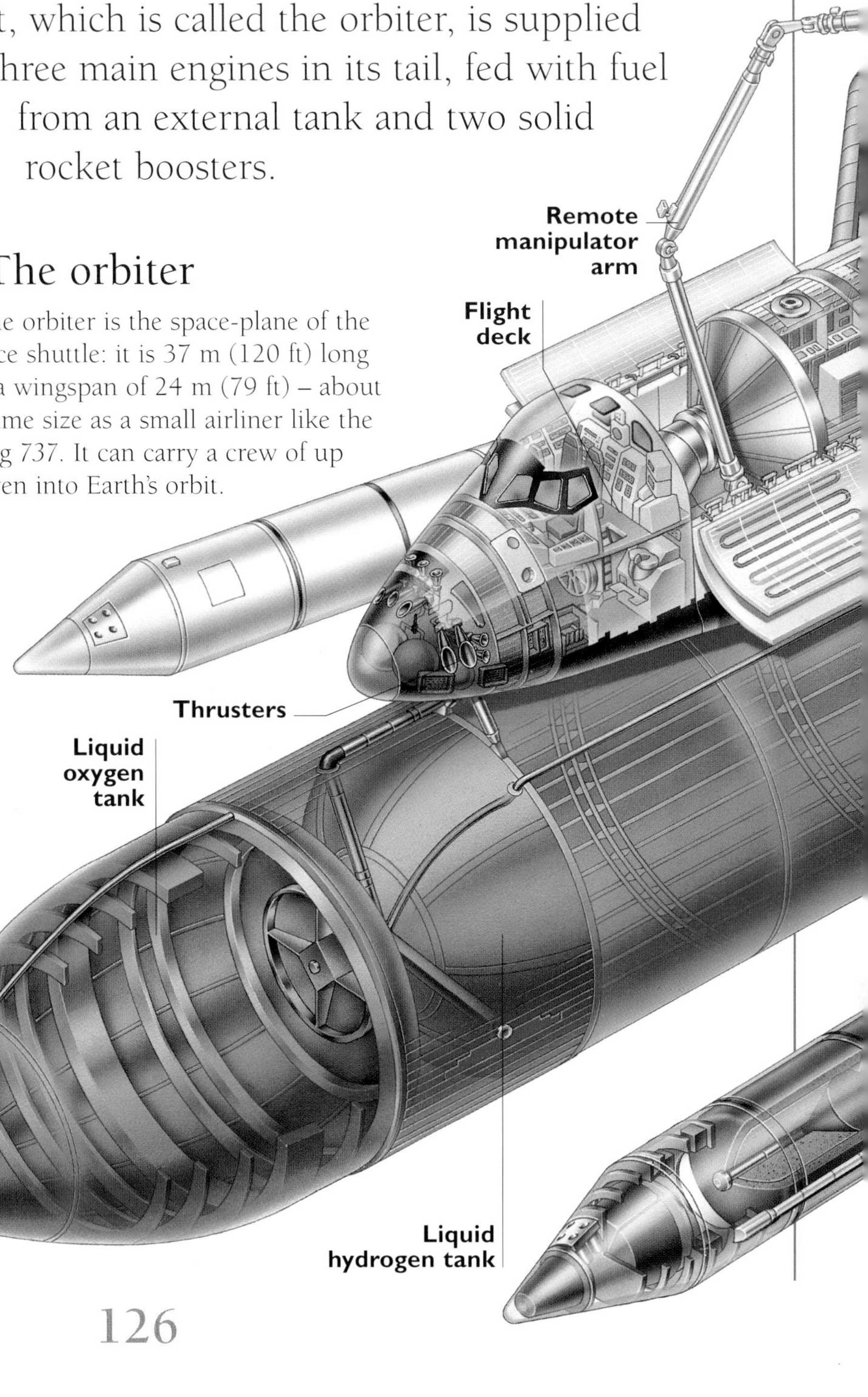

Remote manipulator arm

Flight deck

Thrusters

Liquid oxygen tank

Liquid hydrogen tank

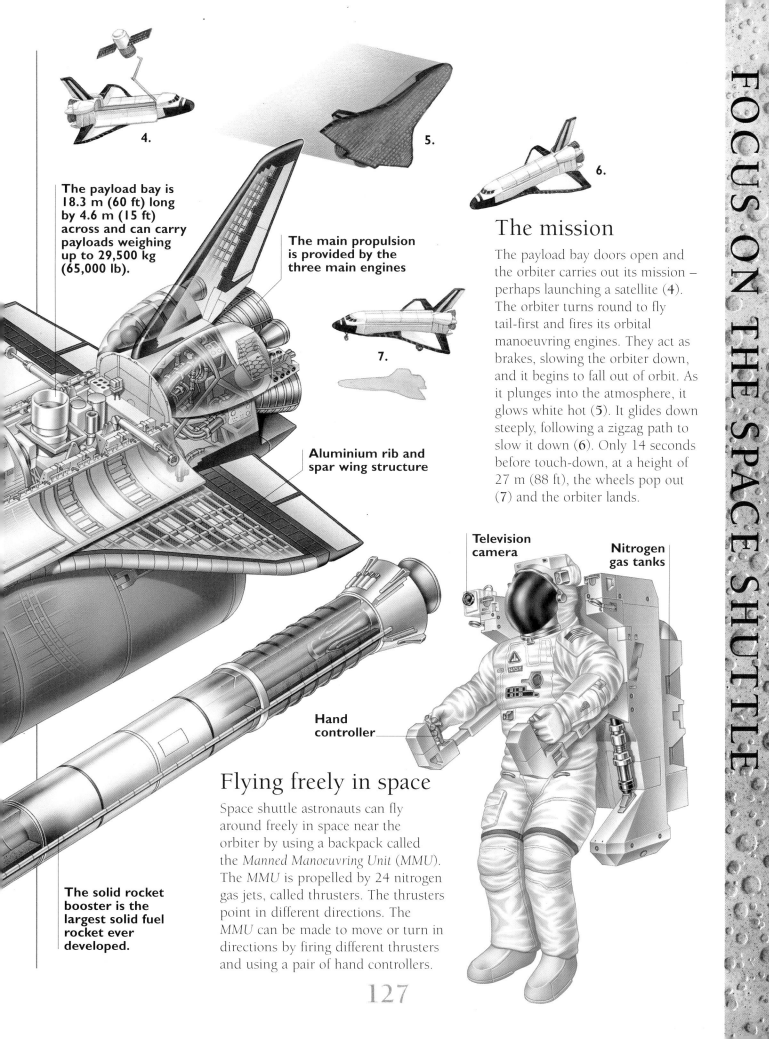

4.

The payload bay is 18.3 m (60 ft) long by 4.6 m (15 ft) across and can carry payloads weighing up to 29,500 kg (65,000 lb).

The main propulsion is provided by the three main engines

5.

6.

7.

Aluminium rib and spar wing structure

The solid rocket booster is the largest solid fuel rocket ever developed.

The mission

The payload bay doors open and the orbiter carries out its mission – perhaps launching a satellite (**4**). The orbiter turns round to fly tail-first and fires its orbital manoeuvring engines. They act as brakes, slowing the orbiter down, and it begins to fall out of orbit. As it plunges into the atmosphere, it glows white hot (**5**). It glides down steeply, following a zigzag path to slow it down (**6**). Only 14 seconds before touch-down, at a height of 27 m (88 ft), the wheels pop out (**7**) and the orbiter lands.

Television camera

Nitrogen gas tanks

Hand controller

Flying freely in space

Space shuttle astronauts can fly around freely in space near the orbiter by using a backpack called the *Manned Manoeuvring Unit* (*MMU*). The *MMU* is propelled by 24 nitrogen gas jets, called thrusters. The thrusters point in different directions. The *MMU* can be made to move or turn in directions by firing different thrusters and using a pair of hand controllers.

127

Space stations

A space station is a large craft that stays in space for several months or years and is visited by different crews. Docking ports allow spacecraft to dock (connect) with the station. Early space stations were launched complete, but larger modern space stations are now launched in pieces and assembled in space. These craft let scientists carry out long-term experiments and observations, for example to study the effects of long space missions on the human body, which will be very important should we one day send people to the planets.

Salyut 1

The first space station, *Salyut* (Russian for "salute") *1* was launched on 19 April 1971 into an orbit 200 km (124 miles) above the Earth. Two *Soyuz* crews (see page 125) visited the craft before it re-entered the atmosphere on 11 October 1971 and burned up. *Salyut 1* carried two telescopes for observing the stars. The cosmonauts carried out medical experiments on each other and studied how plants grow in space.

Country: Russia
Date: 1971
Size: 13 m (42¾ ft)
Construction: aluminium, steel
Top speed: 28,000 km/h (17,500 mph)
On board: Up to 5 crew

Salyut 1

Skylab

Skylab was the first American space station. It was made from an empty fuel tank from a *Saturn* rocket (see page 125). Severe vibration during launch tore off a shield and solar panel, but *Skylab* survived. Three crews each with three astronauts spent 171 days inside it. They took 182,000 photographs of the Sun, 40,000 of the Earth and 2,500 of Comet *Kahoutek*. They also carried out many scientific experiments. The abandoned *Skylab* crashed to Earth in July 1979.

Skylab

Country: USA
Date: 1973
Size: 25.6 m (84 ft)
Construction: aluminium, steel
Top speed: 28,000 km/h (17,500 mph)
On board: 3 crew

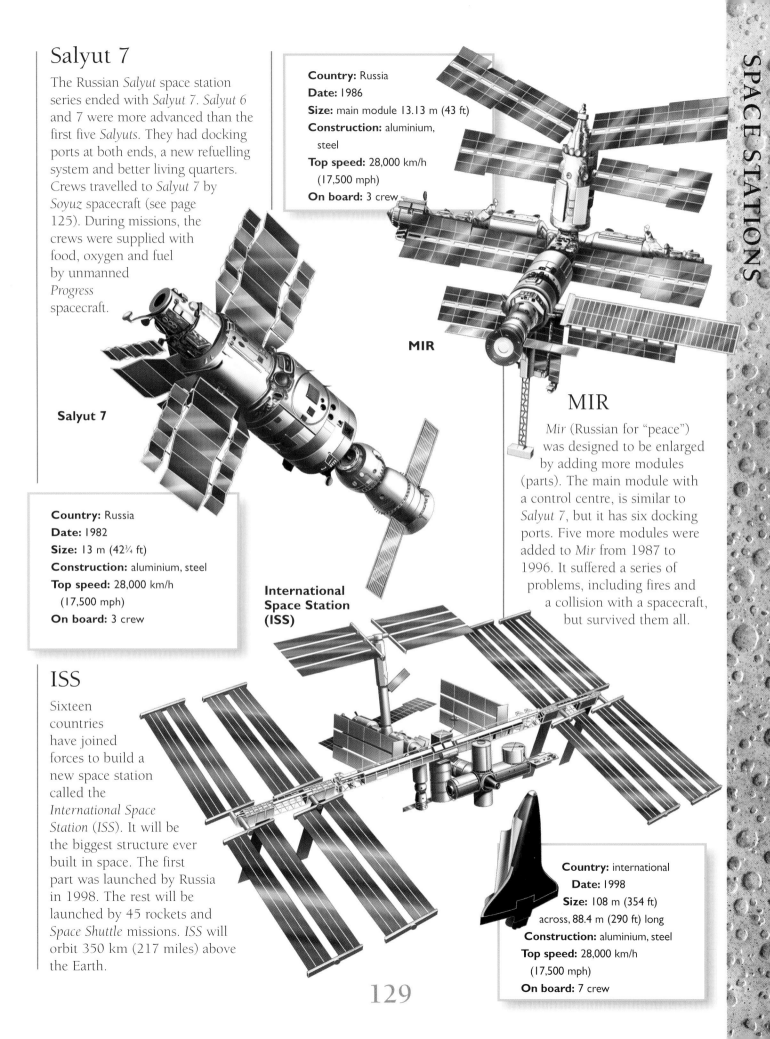

Salyut 7

The Russian *Salyut* space station series ended with *Salyut 7*. *Salyut 6* and 7 were more advanced than the first five *Salyuts*. They had docking ports at both ends, a new refuelling system and better living quarters. Crews travelled to *Salyut 7* by *Soyuz* spacecraft (see page 125). During missions, the crews were supplied with food, oxygen and fuel by unmanned *Progress* spacecraft.

Salyut 7

Country: Russia
Date: 1982
Size: 13 m (42¾ ft)
Construction: aluminium, steel
Top speed: 28,000 km/h (17,500 mph)
On board: 3 crew

Country: Russia
Date: 1986
Size: main module 13.13 m (43 ft)
Construction: aluminium, steel
Top speed: 28,000 km/h (17,500 mph)
On board: 3 crew

MIR

MIR

Mir (Russian for "peace") was designed to be enlarged by adding more modules (parts). The main module with a control centre, is similar to *Salyut 7*, but it has six docking ports. Five more modules were added to *Mir* from 1987 to 1996. It suffered a series of problems, including fires and a collision with a spacecraft, but survived them all.

International Space Station (ISS)

ISS

Sixteen countries have joined forces to build a new space station called the *International Space Station* (*ISS*). It will be the biggest structure ever built in space. The first part was launched by Russia in 1998. The rest will be launched by 45 rockets and *Space Shuttle* missions. *ISS* will orbit 350 km (217 miles) above the Earth.

Country: international
Date: 1998
Size: 108 m (354 ft) across, 88.4 m (290 ft) long
Construction: aluminium, steel
Top speed: 28,000 km/h (17,500 mph)
On board: 7 crew

Into the unknown

Transport in the most remote places and in extreme conditions calls for extraordinary vehicles. Deep-sea explorers travel inside a thick metal sphere that protects them from the crushing water pressure. Scientists who work in the icy polar regions use tracked vehicles to travel across snow. The tracks spread the vehicle's weight and help to stop it from sinking into the snow. The remotest places of all, other worlds, are explored by robot vehicles. They have driven across the Moon and Mars, guided by drivers on Earth linked to the vehicles by radio.

Mathematician David Bushnell's **Turtle** (1776) was a forerunner of the modern submarine. It only carried one man who had to crank the propeller by hand, adjust the water ballast (weight) and steer with very tiny portholes to peer through.

On 23 January 1960, **Jacques Piccard** and **Don Walsh** climbed into their bathyscaphe, **Trieste**, and sank 10,916 m (35,805 ft) to the bottom of the Mariana Trench in the Pacific Ocean. It is still the deepest manned dive ever made.

In 1997, the **Sojourner rover** (*left*) spent 85 days exploring the surface of Mars, studying rocks until its power source failed.

The crews of **Apollo 15**, **16** and **17** took an electric car, the **Apollo lunar rover** (*right*), to the Moon to travel further across the surface than earlier astronauts.

Using a car instead of dogs or horses to pull sleds on his 1907–09 Antarctic expedition was not a success for **Ernest Shackleton**.

The Soviet Union landed two unmanned electric vehicles, **Lunokhod 1** and **2**, on the Moon in the 1970s (*below*). The 756 kg (1,667 lb) vehicles sent 100,000 photographs of the Moon to Earth. They also analysed the strength and chemistry of the Moon's surface.

Timeline of transport

Thousands of years ago, Pacific island fishing boats use outriggers (balancing floats) to keep upright against the currents and winds.

Italian inventor Leonardo da Vinci (1452–1519) sketches the first helicopter and parachute. In 2000 his wooden and canvas parachute is recreated and flies from 6,000 m (20,000 ft).

George and Robert Stephenson's *Rocket* is the first express passenger locomotive reaching a speed of 47 km/h (29 mph).

Karl Benz drives his motorised tricycle in 1885 at the speed of a trotting horse.

1852 Frenchman Henri Giffard flies the first steam airship

1859 Ironclads, warships whose wooden hulls are protected by iron plates, are introduced. The first is the French vessel, *La Gloire*.

1859 Frenchman Etienne Lenoir builds the first internal combustion engine. It is powered by gas.

1863 The first underground railway, with steam locomotives, opens in London.

1869 The USA's Central Pacific and Union Pacific Railroads meet to form the country's first coast-to-coast railway.

1879 The first electric railway is built in Berlin, Germany.

1883 The *Orient Express* train service begins to carry passengers between Paris and Constantinople (modern Istanbul), Turkey.

1885 Carl Benz, a German engineer, builds the world's first petrol-driven car.

1885 The British *Rover* safety bicycle is the first with equal-sized wheels and a chain drive.

1892 German engineer Rudolf Diesel patents a new form of engine which will be named after him.

1897 *Turbinia*, a small turbine-driven steam vessel, breaks speed records. Soon many ships will be powered by turbines.

1903 The Wright brothers make the first powered flights in their aeroplane, *The Flyer*, at Kitty Hawk, North Carolina, USA.

1908 The *Model T Ford*, the most successful of the early mass-produced cars, begins production in the USA.

The first modern-looking bicycles, such as the *Rover*, with chains, spokes and equal-sized inflatable tyres appear in 1885.

The first single-rotor helicopter is developed by Igor Sikorsky in 1939.

1910 The first seaplane is built by French engineer Henri Fabre.

1912 The world's largest liner, *Titanic*, sinks on her maiden voyage when it hits an iceberg.

1914 The Atlantic and Pacific oceans are linked with the opening of the Panama Canal.

1919 British flyers John Alcock and Arthur Whitten-Brown make the first non-stop flight across the Atlantic.

1920 The first aircraft with a retracting undercarriage, the *Dayton-Wright RB* monoplane, is produced.

1923 Aircraft carriers are built for the British and Japanese navies.

1929 Synchromesh, a new design feature on a gearbox, is introduced by the General Motors Corporation. It makes gear-changing much easier.

1933 With the *247*, the Boeing Corporation introduces the first modern airliner.

1936 The Volkswagen *Beetle*, the first "people's car", is designed.

1937 British inventor Frank Whittle builds the world's first jet engine.

1939 The first practical helicopter is designed by Igor Sikorsky.

1947 The American Bell *X-1* rocket plane becomes the first vehicle to break the sound barrier.

1952 The De Havilland Company introduces the *Comet*, the first jet airliner.

1955 The first nuclear-powered submarine, the American *Nautilus*, enters service.

1957 Russia launches *Sputnik I*, the first artificial satellite to orbit the Earth.

The Volkswagen *Beetle* ("People's wagon") is designed by Dr Ferdinand Porsche in 1936. Since then over 20 million of these cars have been sold in 30 countries.

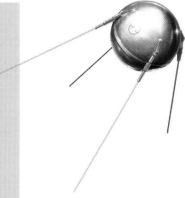

Sputnik I is launched in 1957 and the "space race" begins.

1959 The Austin *Mini* goes on the market.

1959 The first practical hovercraft is demonstrated.

1961 The Soviet spacecraft *Vostok I* carries cosmonaut Yuri Gagarin, the first human to travel into space.

1964 Super-fast "bullet trains" begin to transform travel in Japan.

1969 The American spacecraft *Apollo 11* takes the first astronauts to the Moon.

1969 *Concorde*, the supersonic airliner makes its first test flight.

1969 The Boeing *747*, or jumbo jet, flies for the first time.

1970 *Salyut 1*, the first space station, is orbiting the Earth.

1976 Two unmanned *Viking* spacecraft land on the planet Mars.

1981 The space shuttle *Columbia* makes its first flight.

1981 The French high-speed train, the *TGV*, starts to carry passengers.

1989 The American stealth bomber, the *Northrop B-2*, flies for the first time.

1990 General Motors develops a battery-powered car which could point the way to the future of road transport.

1994 The Channel Tunnel opens, linking Britain and France by rail.

2001 Space station *Mir* re-enters Earth's atmosphere after 15 years in orbit.

The Japanese *Shinkansen*, or *Bullet Train*, has a maximum service speed of 220 km/h (137 mph).

Transport trailblazers

Armstrong, Neil, American astronaut (1930–) Born in Ohio, Armstrong was a pilot and test pilot before being selected as an astronaut in 1962. On 20 July 1969, he was the first person to land on the Moon, speaking the famous words, "That's one small step for [a] man, one giant leap for mankind."

Beebe, Charles, American naturalist and explorer (1877–1962) Beebe was an expert on birds who was also interested in exploring under the sea. Together with engineer Otis Barton he created the bathysphere, a spherical diving vessel which they took to the record depth of 923 m (3,028 ft).

Benz, Karl, German engineer (1844–1929) Benz built the world's first petrol-driven motor car, which took to the road in 1885.

Blériot, Louis, French aviator (1872–1936) Blériot made the first flight across the English Channel on 25 July 1909. He flew a 24-horsepower monoplane that he had built himself.

Braun, Wernher von, German-American rocket scientist (1912–77) Born in Germany, Wernher von Braun developed the *V-2* rocket weapons used during World War II. After the war he moved to the USA, where he worked on the rockets for the first Earth satellites and on the *Saturn* rockets used for the *Apollo* moon-landing.

Campbell, Donald, British racing driver (1921–67) Campbell set several speed records, both on land and on the water, following his father's land-speed record of 280 km/h (174 mph) in 1927. Donald died on Coniston Water in England during his attempt to be the first person to travel at over 300 mph (483 km/h) on water. His own son Donald Wales broke the British land speed record for electric vehicles in 2000 with a speed of 205 km/h (128 mph).

Cayley, George, British scientist (1773–1857) One of the earliest pioneers of aeronautics, Cayley created the first practical glider to carry a person. He realised that powered flight would have to wait until a light but powerful engine could be built.

Cierva, Juan de la, Spanish engineer (1895–1936) Fascinated by flying from an early age, Cierva used his engineering skills to invent and build the autogiro, a forerunner of the helicopter that has both a rotor and an aeroplane propeller.

Cockerell, Christopher, British inventor (1910–2000) Cockerell worked on radar in World War II, but is famous for inventing the hovercraft, a vehicle that rides on a cushion of air. Cockerell had made a working model hovercraft by 1955. Four years later a hovercraft was crossing the English Channel.

Cook, James, British explorer (1728–79) One of the greatest navigators of all time, Cook travelled to the Pacific, sailing along the coasts of Australia, New Zealand and many Pacific islands. He also discovered how to keep people healthy on long voyages. By feeding fresh fruit to his crew, he kept them clear of scurvy, a disease that had plagued sailors for centuries.

Cugnot, Nicholas, French military engineer (1725–1804) Responding to the needs of the army, Cugnot invented a three-wheeled gun carriage that was the first practical steam-driven vehicle. Its top speed was only 3.2 km/h (3 mph), so it did not catch on, and Cugnot had no money to build an improved version.

Daimler, Gottlieb, German inventor (1834–1900) Daimler built a number of improved gas engines before starting work on powered vehicles. In the 1880s he built very early motor cars and motorcycles.

De Havilland, Geoffrey, British aircraft designer (1882–1965) After building his first aircraft himself in 1908, De Havilland ran a company that came up with some of the most successful aircraft of the time. Its 48-seater jet airliner, the *Comet*, was the first of its type, and helped bring about long-distance mass air travel.

Diesel, Rudolf, German engineer (1858–1913) During the 1880s, Rudolf Diesel began work to produce a more efficient internal-combustion engine. He came up with a design in which the fuel ignites at high pressure and which is still widely used in lorries, buses and cars. This type of engine is known as the diesel engine.

Dunlop, John Boyd, Scottish inventor (1840–1921) A Scottish vet working in Belfast, Dunlop fitted his son's tricycle with air-filled rubber tyres in 1887. In doing this, he was reinventing an earlier idea. Dunlop went on to make money from his tyres, founding the Dunlop Rubber Company to make air-filled tyres.

Farman, Henri, French aviator (1874–1958) Farman was one of the first men to fly, piloting the first *Voisin* biplane in 1908. He then went into business to build biplanes, and in 1917 made the *Goliath* bomber, which was converted in 1919 to one of the first airliners.

Ford, Henry, American car manufacturer (1863–1947) Beginning by making cars himself, Ford founded the Ford Motor Company in 1903. Five years later he was producing the *Model T*, the first successful mass-produced car. In all, 15 million *Model T*s were made, bringing motoring within the reach of ordinary Americans.

Fulton, Robert, American inventor (1765–1815) Trained as a painter, Fulton became an engineer during the 1790s. His many inventions included a machine for cutting and polishing marble and a submarine torpedo boat. He is most famous as a pioneer of the steamboat. His vessel *Clermont*, launched on New York's Hudson River in 1806, was the first successful steamer.

Gagarin, Yuri, Russian (Soviet) cosmonaut (1934–68) Gagarin was the first man in space. He orbited the Earth in his spaceship, *Vostok*, in 1961, returning to Earth a Russian hero.

Goddard, Robert, American physicist (1882–1945) One of the greatest pioneers of rocketry, Goddard was little known in his lifetime. He developed the liquid-fuel rocket, built rockets capable of greater and greater speeds, and invented methods of controlling them as they flew. Only after his death was his work recognised.

Goodyear, Charles, American inventor (1800–60) Charles Goodyear spent some 10 years of his life researching and experimenting with rubber. His most important achievement was the invention of vulcanising (toughening rubber by curing with sulphur), without which road vehicle tyres would not have been practical.

Harrison, John, British clock-maker (1693–1776) In 1713 the British government offered a prize for the person who came up with an accurate method of working out longitude at sea. To do this, you need to be able to tell the time, and Harrison set himself the difficult task of making a clock that would be accurate on board ship. He created a series of highly accurate clocks which finally enabled sailors to work out exactly where they were, and, after years of effort, was awarded the prize.

Henry the Navigator, Prince of Portugal (1394–1460) Prince Henry founded a navigation school, set up an observatory, and sent ships across the seas on voyages of exploration. His work paved the way for a great age of sea voyages, during which explorers from Europe were some of the first to visit Africa and America.

Issigonis, Alec, British car designer (1906–88) Born in Turkey, Issigonis moved to Britain in his teens. His most famous design was the *Mini*, which appeared in 1959 and transformed small cars all over the world.

Johnson, Amy, British aviator (1903–41) Amy Johnson was one of the first women to learn to fly. She made many long-distance flights, most famously from England to Australia in 1930.

Jouffroy d'Abbas, Claude, French inventor (1751–1832) The French nobleman Claude Jouffroy d'Abbas built the first really practical steamboat in 1783. However, his work was ignored until steamboats were taken up by inventors like Robert Fulton.

Lenoir, Étienne, French engineer (1822–1900) The internal combustion engine was invented by French engineer Étienne Lenoir. Lenoir's original engine was fuelled by coal gas, but later versions were used in petrol-powered cars and aeroplanes.

Lilienthal, Otto, German inventor (1849–96) Lilienthal was a great pioneer of the glider and made many flights in craft that he built himself. He studied the flight of birds, hoping to build a flying machine with flapping wings. Lilienthal fell to his death during one of his flights.

McAdam, John, Scottish engineer (1756–1836) McAdam had a career in business in the USA before settling back in Scotland to invent a better way of building roads. He developed a hard-wearing road surface using gravel and crushed stone, and raised them so that they drained properly. The word "tarmac" is derived from this inventor's name.

Messerschmidt, Willy, German aircraft manufacturer (1898–1978) During the mid-20th century, Messerschmidt's company produced aircraft such as the *Me.109*, the fastest aeroplane in the world in 1939, and the *Me.262*, the first jet aircraft to fly in World War II.

Montgolfier brothers, French balloonists Joseph Michel (1740–1810) and Jacques Étienne Montgolfier (1745–99) These brothers constructed the first hot-air balloon in 1782. In 1783 they launched the first manned balloon flight, taking two of their friends some 915 m (3,000 ft) high.

Olds, Ransom, American car manufacturer (1864–1950) After trying steam-powered cars, Ransom Olds began to make petrol-driven Oldsmobiles in 1899. Later he pioneered the assembly-line method of production, which was taken up even more successfully by Henry Ford.

Otto, Nikolaus, German engineer (1832–91) Otto was a pioneer of the internal combustion engine. He invented the four-stroke cycle, the principle still used in car engines today.

Parsons, Charles, Irish engineer (1854–1931) After training as an engineer, Parsons developed the high-speed steam turbine, a device that transformed ship propulsion and electricity generation. He first became famous when his turbine-driven steamship, the *Turbinia*, broke all speed records.

Plimsoll, Samuel, British politician (1824–98) A member of the British Parliament, Samuel Plimsoll was concerned about the safety of overloaded merchant ships which sat too low in the water. He introduced a mark, which was painted on the hull of every merchant ship, showing the point down to which the ship could be loaded. This mark is still called the Plimsoll line.

Porsche, Ferdinand, German car designer (1875–1951) Porsche began as a designer for German companies such as Daimler before he went on to design the famous Volkswagen *Beetle*, and later the *Porsche* sports car.

Pullman, George, American businessman (1831–97) The luxurious Pullman sleeping car was patented in 1864 and 1865, after which George Pullman founded a company to produce and sell his invention. Pullman also invented the railway dining car and devised a way of connecting railway coaches with covered passages.

Royce, Henry, British engineer (1863–1933) Royce was an electrical engineer who became interested in cars. He made his first car in 1904 and his work so impressed Charles Rolls (1877–1910) that they joined to form Rolls-Royce, making luxury cars and aircraft engines.

Sikorsky, Igor, Russian-American engineer (1889–1972) While a young man, Sikorsky wanted to produce a craft that could take off vertically, so he came up with the idea of the helicopter, with its spinning rotor. He made his first successful helicopter in 1939 and all later helicopters have been based on this design.

Stephenson, British engineers, George (1781–1848) and his son Robert (1803–59) George and Robert were important railway pioneers. They worked together on the Stockton and Darlington and Liverpool and Manchester railways, and on the famous locomotive, the *Rocket*, which set new standards for both speed and reliability.

Tereshkova, Valentina, Russian (Soviet) cosmonaut (1937–) The first woman to fly in space, Valentina Tereshkova, piloted the spacecraft *Vostok 6* in 1963. She completed 48 Earth orbits in her three-day flight.

Trevithick, Richard, British engineer (1771–1833) Richard Trevithick worked as a mining engineer and made several steam road vehicles before building the first steam railway locomotives.

Westinghouse, George, American inventor (1846–1914) Amongst Westinghouse's many inventions in the field of engineering, the most famous was the air brake. This allowed a train driver to control the brakes on all the train's carriages at once. This made trains safer and able to go at higher speeds.

Whittle, Frank, British engineer (1907–96) While a student, Whittle began the research which led to the jet engine. His work was ignored by the authorities, but he carried on, patenting his first jet engine in 1930. By 1941, a British jet-powered aircraft, a *Gloster E28/39*, was in the air.

Wright, American pioneers of flying, Orville (1871–1948) and Wilbur (1867–1912) The Wright brothers made the first powered flight ever, in their own-designed glider.

Zeppelin, Count Ferdinand von, German airship manufacturer (1838–1917) Zeppelin was an army officer who became interested in flight. He made his first airship in 1900. Soon, whenever people thought of airships, they thought of Zeppelin.

Transport record breakers

On wheels

First car
The first petrol-engine car was built by Karl Benz of Mannheim, Germany, in 1885 (see page 12). It was a three-wheeler and could travel at about 13 km/h (8 mph).

Most popular cars
The first really popular car was the *Model T Ford* (see page 18), which was made from 1908 to 1927. In that time around 15 million *Model Ts* were made. They are still being driven today by car enthusiasts. But more Volkswagen *Beetles* (see page 18) were produced than any other type of car. When production in Germany stopped in the early 1970s, there were over 16 million *Beetles*.

Most economical vehicle
Probably the best fuel consumption figures to date were achieved by a vehicle designed by *Honda* during a contest in Finland in 1996. The *Honda* managed 3,336 km/litre (417 mpg) – 10 times better than many standard family cars.

Fastest car
The world's fastest car is *Thrust SSC* (see page 14), which is powered by two jet engines. *Thrust SSC*, driven by Andy Green

of Britain, was the first car to go faster than the speed of sound.

Fastest racing car
The racing cars that travel fastest are drag racers (see page 14), which move from standing to speeds of over 500 km/h (310 mph) on a course of just 402 m (1,320 ft). The world record was set by American driver Gary Scelzi, who reached 522.3 km/h (326½ mph) in 1998.

Fastest production car
The *McLaren F1* is the fastest car that can be driven on the road. It is capable of speeds of up to 386.7 km/h (240 mph) and can accelerate from 0 to 96 km/h (60 mph) in a little over three seconds.

Longest car
People often try to build cars that are long enough to beat the world record. These

Peterbilt truck

Ferrari 250 GTO

machines are so long that they are not practical road-going vehicles – but they make interesting displays at fairs and exhibitions. Probably the longest to date measures 30.5 m (100 ft) and was designed by Jay Ohrberg. The American vehicle has 24 wheels and there is a small swimming pool, complete with a diving board, in the rear.

Longest bicycle
The longest modern bicycle was made during the 1980s, measuring 22.2 m (73 ft) long, and was ridden by four people. But in the late 19th century a 10-person bicycle, called *La Décuplette*, was built in France.

Fastest cyclist
Some cyclists have travelled faster than most people have ever managed in a car. This is because a cycle can pick up speed when travelling in the slipstream of another powered vehicle. The fastest to date was the Dutch cyclist Fred Rompelberg, who clocked up an amazing 268.8 km/h (167 mph) in 1995.

On water

First round-the-world
Portuguese navigator Ferdinand Magellan embarked with five ships to sail around the world in 1519. During the journey Magellan and most of his crew of 260 men died, but in 1522 one of his ships with 18 aboard completed the voyage.

First across the Atlantic
The first likely sailors to have crossed the Atlantic were Viking seamen in around 1001. This was the year when Leif the Lucky, son of Erik the Red, first set foot on the country he called Vinland, which was probably Newfoundland, Canada.

Galleon

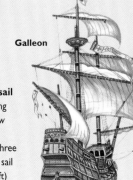

Fastest under sail
The swiftest sailing vessel is the *Yellow Pages Endeavour*, a trimaran with three short hulls and a sail that is 12 m (40 ft)

high. In 1993 the vessel managed a speed of 86.2 km/h (46½ knots) at Sandy Point, Australia.

First submarine strike
The *Hunley*, a Confederate submarine, sunk a Union sloop in 1864, during the American Civil War (1861–65). It rammed a torpedo attached to a harpoon-like bow into the enemy's wooden hull, released a 45-m (150-ft) rope, withdrew and then tightened the rope to activate the explosive. It was not until World War I (1914–18) that another submarine sank a ship in battle.

Water speed record
The hydroplane *Spirit of Australia* set the water speed record in 1978. The craft, driven by Ken Warby, reached a speed of 511.1 km/h (276 knots). However, Warby accelerated to about 555 km/h (300 knots) on another occasion the previous year, but officials were not present to witness the record.

Biggest warships
The world's largest warships are aircraft carriers owned by the US Navy. They are seven *Nimitz Class* carriers, the biggest of which are 333 m (1,092 ft) long. These vast floating runways can carry almost 100 aircraft.

Biggest submarines
The largest submarines ever built belonged to the Russian *Typhoon* class. *Typhoons* are 172 m (563 ft) in length, are powered by twin nuclear reactors and can travel at 46 km/h (25 knots) when submerged.

Biggest cargo ships
The *Jahre Viking* of Norway is the world's largest ship. The vessel is a supertanker and is 458 m (1,503 ft) in length and 69 m (226 ft) wide. It takes about five minutes to walk from the bow (front) of the ship to the stern (rear).

Container capacity
Big container ships can carry up to 2,700 separate containers. If you stacked them all one on top of the other, they would reach the height of Mount Everest.

Longest yachts
Abdul Aziz, the yacht of the Saudi Arabian royal family, is 147 m (482 ft) long.

Rowing the Atlantic
In 1997, two New Zealanders, Phil Stubbs and Robert Hamill, rowed across the Atlantic Ocean in 41 days, beating the previous record by 32 days.

On the tracks

Largest steam engine
The biggest, heaviest and most powerful steam locomotives in the world are the "Big Boys" (see page 81). The enormous engines weigh around 500 tonnes and were built to pull freight trains across Utah in the USA. The locomotives were 40 m (131¼ ft) long, and the driving wheel was 1.8 m (5¾ ft) in diameter. The firebox alone was large enough for a family dining room.

Fastest steam engine
The British *Mallard* (see page 81), with its sleek streamlined body, is the fastest-ever steam locomotive. In 1938, it reached 201 km/h (126 mph) on a special journey along the main line between London and Edinburgh.

SD40-2

Largest diesel engine
The longest diesel engines run in the USA. They work on the Union Pacific Railway, are almost 30 m (100 ft) long and weigh 229 tonnes.

Largest freight train
Probably the longest ever freight train was made up of 500 coal wagons and ran on Ohio's Norfolk and Western Railroad, USA, in 1967. The train was pulled by six diesel locomotives and was 6.4 km (4 miles) in length.

Longest rail tunnel
The world's longest railway tunnel connects the Japanese islands of Honshu and Hokkaido. The tunnel is 53 km (33 miles) long, and most of it runs under water.

Largest railway station
New York's Grand Central Station is the world's largest. It has 44 platforms.

Widest track
Some of the world's widest trains run on track with a gauge (width) of 1.676 m (5½ ft). This gauge is used in China, India, Pakistan, Spain, Portugal and Argentina.

Fastest modern train
Of the world's various high-speed train services, the current record-holder is a French *TGV* (*Train à Grande Vitesse*). In 1990, the *TGV* (see page 86) reached 515 km/h (320 mph) near Vendôme. In normal service, however, *TGVs* run more slowly, with speeds averaging 212 km/h (132 mph) along much of the Paris-Lyon route.

In the air

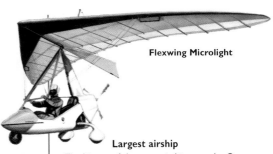
Flexwing Microlight

First transatlantic solo flight
Charles Lindbergh, a pilot from Detroit, USA, made the first solo transatlantic flight in 1927. The journey took just 33 hours in Lindbergh's Ryan monoplane, *The Spirit of St Louis*. The first non-stop transatlantic crossing (from Newfoundland to Ireland) had been achieved by British pilots John Alcock and Arthur Brown in 1919.

Fastest aircraft
The fastest aircraft of all was the *Lockheed SR-71* of 1964. Its top speed was 3,530 km/h (2,193 mph) and it was said to be able to fly as high as 30,000 m (98,000 ft).

Fastest airliner
The BAC/Aérospatiale *Concorde* is the world's fastest airliner (see page 107). It reaches 2,333 km/h (1,450 mph) – 2.2 times the speed of sound.

Biggest aircraft
The Airbus Super Transport *A300-600 Beluga* is the world's largest cargo-carrying aircraft. Its vast cargo compartment has a volume of 1,400 sq m (49,440 sq ft) and a length of 37.7 m (124 ft).

Biggest wingspan
The aeroplane with the longest wingspan was the *Hughes H4 Hercules*, a flying boat that was also nicknamed the "Spruce Goose". This massive aircraft, which was intended for the US government by American businessman Howard Hughes, had a wingspan of 97.5 m (320 ft). The plane, which cost $40 million to build, was only flown for a single test flight.

Largest airship
The biggest of the great airships was the German hydrogen-filled *Hindenburg*. Completed in March 1936, the *Hindenburg* took 10 days to travel around the world and made some 20 crossings of the Atlantic before it caught fire in May 1937, killing many of those on board.

Smallest aeroplane
The smallest working, human-piloted aeroplane was *Bumble Bee Two*. This tiny single-seater was just 2.7 m (9 ft) long and had a wingspan of 1.7 m (5.5 ft). The plane, built by Robert Tempe of Arizona, crashed in 1988.

Human-powered flight
In 1979, the first successful human-powered series, the *Gossamer Albatross*, flew across the English Channel. The flight finally fulfilled a dream of human-powered flight that had begun with the first experimental flying machines of the 19th century.

First strap-on personal helicopter
This could be the *SoloTrek* currently being developed with help from NASA (the American space agency). It straps on to the back of the wearer to fly at speeds of 120 km/h (75 mph) over a range of (250 km) 155 miles.

In space

First living creature in space
The first live creature in space was not a person but a dog. The animal, called Laika, went into space in the Russian *Sputnik 2* in 1957, shortly after the launch of *Sputnik 1*, the first artificial earth-orbiting satellite.

Shortest space flight
In May 1961, the American astronaut Alan Shepard made the briefest manned space flight on board *Freedom 7*. Shepard's spacecraft did not go into orbit, but flew in a huge curve, landing some 15 minutes after it took off. But it did leave the Earth's atmosphere, and made Shepard the second man in space after Russia's Yuri Gagarin.

First space probe on another planet
The Russian probe *Venera 7* was the first space probe to land on another planet. The craft landed on the planet Venus in 1970.

Fastest speed
The fastest-ever speed reached by a human being is 39,897 km/h (24,791 mph). It was achieved by the American astronauts of *Apollo 10* when they returned to Earth in May 1969.

Longest continuous time in space
Russian Valeriy Poliyakov spent 437 days, 17 hours, 58 minutes and 16 seconds from January 1994 to March 1995 on two *Soyuz* spacecrafts and the space station, *Mir* (see page 129).

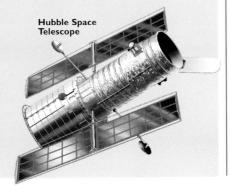
Hubble Space Telescope

Glossary of transport terms

Accelerator
A control, usually a pedal on a car, that allows you to increase or reduce the speed of the engine.

Aerodynamics
The study of the movement of objects through a gas; in road transport, usually used to cut down friction and make vehicles more efficient.

Aft
Towards the rear of a vessel or aircraft.

Aileron
Flap on an aeroplane wing that the pilot can move to cause the aircraft to roll left or right and enter a turn.

Air brakes
Brakes that work using compressed air, used by trucks and trains.

Airbag
Safety device in a car, consisting of a bag that inflates with air to provide a cushion for the driver or passengers in a crash.

Air-cushion vehicle
A hovercraft that glides over land or water on a layer of compressed air.

Airship
Lighter-than-air aircraft with a gas-filled balloon-like envelope, an engine and a steering mechanism.

Alcohol
Used in many rockets as a fuel; and, in Brazil, as an alternative fuel to petrol to run cars.

Alloy
Substance made by mixing two or more metals to improve strength or hardness.

Amphibious
Capable of travelling both on land and in water.

Articulated
Containing a joint; an articulated lorry has its front section joined to the rear by a flexible link that makes it easy to manoeuvre.

Axle
Rod passing through the centre of a wheel, allowing the wheel to turn.

Barge
A flat-bottomed vessel, mainly for carrying freight, used mostly on rivers and canals; also a ceremonial boat.

Barque
Three- or four-masted ship with the mizzen- (rear) mast rigged with sails positioned fore-and-aft and the other masts square-rigged.

Barquentine
Three-masted ship with the main- and mizzen- (rear) masts fore-and-aft rigged, and the fore-mast square rigged.

BHP   *See* brake horsepower.

Biplane
Aeroplane with twin wings, one above the other.

Blimp
Small airship that does not have a rigid frame, often used for advertising.

Boat
Any small, water-going vessel, powered by oars, sails or motor.

Boiler
Container in which water is boiled to produce steam in a steam engine.

Brake horsepower (BHP)
Unit of measurement of the effective power of an engine, measured by working out the force applied to a brake by the engine drive shaft in a special testing machine (*see also* horsepower).

Bridge
Place on a ship from which the captain controls the vessel.

Broadside
All the guns of a ship that can be fired together in the same direction.

Buggy
Lightweight horse-drawn carriage; or small vehicle used for recreation.

Bulkhead
Dividing partition wall inside a ship or aircraft.

Bullet train
Very fast bullet-nosed train as used on the Japanese *Shinkansen* network.

Cab
Part of a lorry or railway engine that accommodates the driver.

Caravel
Light sailing ship used between the 14th and 17th centuries.

Carbon fibre
Very strong, lightweight material used in making many items related to transport, from turbine blades to high-performance boats.

Cargo
Goods carried by a lorry, merchant ship or freight train.

Carrack
Large trading ship used between the 14th and 16th centuries.

Catamaran
Ship or boat with twin hulls.

Chassis
Supporting frame and wheels of a motor vehicle or carriage.

Clipper
Tall-masted cargo-carrying sailing ship of the 19th century, capable of very fast sea journeys.

Cockpit
Part of an aircraft, spacecraft, racing car and powerboat where the captain, pilot or driver sits.

Cog
North European cargo ship of the Middle Ages with a single mast and square sail.

Commuter train
Train used by people travelling to work, usually from the outskirts to the centre of a large city.

Composites
Plastics, such as carbon fibre which are used in vehicle construction. Alloys, which are also used, are metals.

Conning tower
Upward-pointing structure on a submarine used for navigation and as the entrance to the vessel.

Container
A standard-sized steel box used on many ships, trucks and trains for carrying cargo.

Convertible
Car with a roof, often made of fabric, that can be folded back or taken off.

Corsair
Pirate, especially one from North Africa; or the vessel sailed by such a person.

Coupé
Two-door car with a roof that has a marked downward slope towards the back.

Cow-catcher
Structure on the front of a railway locomotive designed to sweep obstructions off the track.

Craft
General term for any ship or boat, or any air or space vehicle.

Crew
Group of people who work on board a ship or aircraft, under the command of the captain.

Cylinder
Tube-shaped part of an engine, in which a piston moves up and down.

Deck
One of the horizontal floors of a ship or aircraft.

Derailleur
Gearing system used on bicycles, in which the chain can be shifted from one drive cog to another.

Diesel engine
Type of internal combustion engine in which the fuel ignites because it is injected directly into the cylinder when the air has been compressed to high pressure.

Dirigible
Craft, usually an airship, that can be steered, rather than just drifting like a free balloon.

Drag
The force that tends to slow down any vehicle travelling through air or water.

Engine
Mechanical device that powers a ship, car, train or other vehicle.

Estate
Car with a rear-door opening on to an area behind the seats designed to carry luggage or other goods.

Exhaust
Waste gases produced by an engine. Also, the part of the engine through which the waste emissions pass.

Ferry
Vessel that carries passengers (and often vehicles) back and forth across a stretch of water.

Fibreglass
Lightweight material made by moulding a mat or cloth of thin glass fibres in a plastic matrix. Used in some car bodies and the hulls of some boats; also called glass-fibre or GRP (glass reinforced plastic).

Fore
Towards the front of a vessel or aircraft.

Four-stroke cycle
Most petrol and diesel engines operate on this cycle of strokes (the up and down movements) of the pistons.

Four-wheel drive (4WD)
Type of motor vehicle in which the power of the engine is transferred to all four wheels (rather than the standard two), to provide good traction on difficult ground.

Freight
Cargo or goods. A freighter is a cargo vessel.

Friction
Resistance felt when one surface rubs against another.

Galleon
Large sailing ship with high fore and after castles, used in the 15th and 16th centuries.

Gallon
Non-metric measurement of capacity equivalent to approximately 4.5 litres.

Gauge
Measurement of the distance between a pair of railway wheels or rails. This varies around the world: the standard gauge in North America, most of Western Europe and China is 143.5 cm (56½ in).

Gears
System of cogs that transmits the motion of the engine to the wheels of a motor vehicle and which can change the speed and torque available.

Glider
Aircraft designed in a similar way to an aeroplane, but without an engine. Very efficient aerodynamic design allows it to stay airborne using natural upcurrents.

Hatchback
Car with a sloping rear door that opens upwards.

Haul
To pull, to transport or (of a ship) to change direction.

Helium
A very light, chemically inert gas often used in airships.

Horsepower (HP)
Measurement of power, roughly equivalent to the strength of one horse.

Hovercraft
Vessel supported by a cushion of air, capable of travelling over land and sea.

HPV (Human Powered Vehicle)
Any human-powered transport including bicycle-style vehicles.

Hull
Body of a ship.

Hydrofoil
Vessel fitted with wing-like structures under the hull called foils that develop lift and raise the hull out of the water as it travels.

Hydrogen
A very light, highly-flammable gas which is and was once used in balloons and airships.

Jet engine
Engine that uses the momentum of a jet of hot exhaust gas to propel an aeroplane or other vehicle.

Juggernaut
A term (of Hindu origin) now used to describe a very large truck.

Jumbo jet
Large, wide-bodied airliner.

Jump jet
Fighter aeroplane that can take off and land vertically.

Keel
Main structural part of a ship that stretches along the whole of the bottom of the vessel; it may also protrude down into the water to help make the vessel more stable.

Kilowatt
Unit of power now replacing horsepower in automotive engineering.

Knot
Measurement of speed equivalent to 1.853184 km/h (1 nautical mile per hour).

Lift
Force needed to raise an aircraft into the air.

Liner
Large vessel that carries passengers.

Litre
Standard metric measurement of capacity.

Locomotive
The engine unit of a railway train.

Mach
A measurement of an aircraft's speed compared to the speed of sound. Mach 1 means the plane is travelling at the speed of sound; Mach 2 means twice the speed of sound. At sea level the speed of sound is 1,220 km/h (758 mph) but it is slower the higher you go.

Machine gun
Automatic gun that can fire many bullets at high speed, attached to tanks, fighter aircraft, bombers and other military vehicles. Also carried by infantry.

Magnet
Piece of iron that attracts other metals containing iron.

Manoeuvre
Intricate movement of vehicle that requires skill to achieve.

Marshalling yard
Area containing many linked railway tracks, where railway wagons are sorted and joined together to form trains.

Mass production
Method of making objects in large numbers using standard, repetitive processes, as with the modern motor car.

Mast
Vertical structure or pole that carries a ship's sails, or other equipment in powered vessels.

Merchant ship
Vessel designed to carry goods, particularly from one country to another.

Metro
Underground railway system serving a town or city. Also called subway in USA.

Microlight
Very small, lightweight aeroplane.

Module
Single part that can be interchanged with other parts of the same size.

Monorail
Railway that travels on a single rail.

Nozzle
Outlet tube or spout; pipe through which fuel enters a cylinder in an internal combustion engine. Also exit zone of jet or rocket engine.

Nuclear power
Power generated as a result of a nuclear reaction. The heat of the nuclear reaction is used to create steam and drive a turbine.

Orbit
Circular path around a planet or moon followed by a spacecraft or satellite, or by one astronomical body around another.

Outrigger
Stabilizing framework or structure sticking out from one side of a boat; or, a boat with such a structure to increase stability.

Oxidiser
Chemical supplied to a rocket engine that helps the fuel to burn.

Paddle
Short oar, normally used in a canoe.

Pantograph
Metal framework fitted on top of an electric locomotive or tram, to collect current from overhead wires.

Piston
Cylindrical component that moves up and down inside the cylinder of an engine.

Pneumatic tyre
Vehicle tyre filled with compressed air.

Probe
Vehicle used for space exploration; particularly an unmanned vehicle sent to one of the planets or to travel outside the solar system.

Propeller
Device made up of a shaft and several specially shaped blades, used to drive a ship or aeroplane; also called a screw.

Prototype
The first finished example of a vehicle, built as a one-off, before regular production begins and from which later examples can be copied.

Pullman
Railway carriage with comfortable accommodation for both sitting and for sleeping.

Rack and pinion
Steering mechanism used in many cars, in which a toothed wheel (the pinion) engages with a toothed bar (the rack).

Radar
System that uses reflected radio waves to detect invisible objects, such as aircraft in the sky or ships at sea; it is also used by pilots and sailors to work out their own position. The word radar comes from the phrase "Radio Detection And Ranging".

Reconnaissance
A first survey of an area to learn its features; air forces or navies may use specialised reconnaissance aircraft or ships to check for enemy positions.

Rickshaw
Small carriage with two wheels, pulled by a person or by someone riding a bicycle.

Rig
The arrangement of sails on a boat or ship.

Rigging
The ropes that hold up a ship's masts and control its sails.

Rolling stock
Railway vehicles – including locomotives, carriages and goods wagons.

Rotor
Arrangement of spinning blades fitted to a helicopter.

Rudder
Moveable flap for steering a boat or aircraft.

Rush hour
Time when most people are travelling to and from work, school and so on.

Saloon
Cabin on a boat where people relax and eat their meals; or an enclosed car with front and rear seats.

Satellite
Object that orbits a planet.

Schooner
Two-masted ship, with sails rigged fore-and-aft.

Ship
Any large, sea-going vessel.

Shunting
Moving railway rolling stock from one line to another.

Skidoo
Vehicle used in snow, with caterpillar tracks at the rear and steerable skis at the front.

Sledge
Vehicle with sliding runners, usually used to travel across snow, also called a sleigh.

Smokestack
Chimney of a steam locomotive.

Solar power
Energy generated using the rays of the sun.

Stacking
System whereby air traffic control keeps planes waiting to land, circling above at fixed heights.

Stratosphere
Part of the atmosphere, beginning from 8–16 km (5–10 miles) above the Earth's surface.

Streamlined
Designed with a sleek, aerodynamic body, so that drag is kept low.

Submersible
Small submarine used for exploration and other non-military work.

Supersonic
Faster than the speed of sound.

Suspension
System of springs and other devices that support a vehicle's body on its axles and is designed to cushion those travelling inside from bumps on the ground.

Tailplane
Flat part of an aircraft's tail, designed to make the craft more stable in flight.

Tanker
Vessel or vehicle in which most of the body is made up of large tanks for carrying liquids in bulk.

Tender
Rear part of a steam locomotive, carrying supplies of coal and water.

Thermals
Currents of warm air on which gliders soar.

Thrust
Pushing force produced by a jet engine or rocket that moves the craft forwards.

Tiller
Lever used to control a boat's rudder.

Tolls
Barriers with booths collecting payments to use a stretch of road, canal or bridge.

Tonne
Metric measurement of weight virtually the same as a ton (1 tonne = 0.98420 tons).

Torpedo
Self-propelled underwater weapon which explodes when it hits the target.

Tram
Passenger-carrying vehicle that runs along rails on a road.

Transmission
System (consisting of gearbox and clutch) that transfers power from a motor vehicle's engine to its wheels.

Trolley
Device, fitted to a trolleybus, that collects electric power from overhead wires.

Tug
Ship that tows other vessels.

Turbine
Motor which uses a bladed wheel that is turned by the force of water, steam or burning gas.

Turbo (turbocharger)
Type of turbine fitted to a vehicle engine; it supplies air under pressure to the engine's cylinders for better performance.

Turbofan
Jet engine that uses a large fan to increase the thrust at lower speeds suited to civil aircraft.

Turbojet
Gas turbine engine which propels an aircraft by its high-speed exhaust. A turboprop powers a propeller.

Vessel
Any ship, boat or water-borne transport.

Wagon
Railway truck for carrying freight; or, a four-wheeled horse-drawn vehicle, especially for carrying goods.

Wind tunnel
Device for producing a steady stream of air, used for testing the aerodynamics of cars, aircraft and other vehicles.

Wingspan
Tip-to-tip length of an aircraft's wings.

Index

Acknowledgements

Kinsey & Harrison would like to thank:

John W. Walker, Director at TAL Management Ltd., Hampshire, England (for Cable & Wireless Adventurer); Tim Cley at Reynard Motorsports Ltd, Oxon (for Indy cars); Bart Garbrecht, President at CEO P.R.O.P. Tour, Inc., Lake Hamilton, Florida, USA (for F1 powerboats); Cameron Kellegher at HSBC and Jaguar Racing (for F1 cars); Ford/Pivco Industries AS (for Th!nk car); Pegasus Aviation; Jason Lewis at www.goals.com; Robert Dane and Mark Gold at www.solarsailor.com.

Artwork credits

t = top; b = bottom; l = left; r = right; c = centre

Tony Bryan: 30–31; 34–35; 104–5; 106–7; 108–9; 112–13. Peter Bull: 12–13, 46–47; 48–49; 50–51; 52–53; 54–55; 58–59; 60–61; 64–65; 66–67; 68–69; 70–71; 72b; 76–77; 86–87; 100–101; 102–103; 111tl; 116b; 130c. Mark Franklin: 8–9; 10–11; 14–15; 16–17; 18–19; 20–21; 22–23; 24–25; 28–29; 32–33; 36–37; 126–27. John James: 56–57; 110–11 (except tl); 126l; 127t. John Lawson: 26–27; 62–63. Simon Roulstone: 38–39; 40–41; 78–79; 80–81; 82–83; 84–85; 88–89; 90–91; 92–93; 94–95; 114–15; 120–21; 122–23; 124–25; 128–29. Peter Sarson: 130tr.

Photographic Credits

t = top; b = bottom; l = left; r = right; c = centre

6/7 Robert Harding Picture Library/Ian Griffiths; 26 AllSport/Mark Thompson; 42l Corbis/Hulton Deutsch Collection, 42/43t Science & Society Picture Library/Science Museum, 42/43b Science & Society Picture Library/Science Museum, 43t,c Bryan & Cherry Alexander, 43b Dyson Industries Ltd; 44/45 The Stock Market; 63 Ajax Silver Image Picture Library; 72l Popperfoto, 72r Corbis/Bettmann, 73t Kos Picture Source, 73c Seaco Picture Library, 73b Kos Picture Source; 74/75 The Stock Market; 86 Milepost 921/2; 96l Corbis/Nik Wheeler, 96r Ford/Pirco Industries AS, 96/97t Solar Sailor/Cannings Australia, 96/97b Popperfoto/Mark Baker, 97 Corbis/Michael S. Yamashita; 98/99 Robert Harding Picture Library; 100 NASA; 102 Corbis/Bettmann; 116 gettyone Stone, 117tl Milepost 921/2/Colin Garratt, 117tr Corbis/Roger Wood 117bl Corbis/Gunter Marx, 117br Corbis/Neil Beer; 118/119, 126 NASA; 130 Popperfoto/NASA, 130/131 Royal Geographical Society, 131t NASA, 131b Novosti (London).

Every effort has been made to trace the copyright holders. Marshall Editions apologises for any unintentional omissions and would be pleased, in such cases, to add an acknowledgement in future editions.